RÉSUMÉS
FOR
BETTER
JOBS

Lawrence D. Brennan, Ph.D.

Communication Consultant, Author, and Lecturer

Stanley Strand, M.A.

Seton Hall University

Edward C. Gruber, Ph.D.

Author, Editor, and Lecturer

MONARCH PRESS

Copyright © 1973, 1981 by
SIMON & SCHUSTER

All rights reserved. No part of this book may be reproduced in any form without permission in writing
from the publisher.

Published by
MONARCH PRESS
a Simon & Schuster division of
Gulf & Western Corporation
Simon & Schuster Building
1230 Avenue of the Americas
New York, N.Y. 10020

MONARCH PRESS and colophon are trademarks of Simon
& Schuster, registered in the U.S. Patent and Trade-
mark Office.

ISBN: 0-671-18708-2

20 19 18 17 16 15 14

Printed in the United States of America

Contents

INTRODUCTION

RESUMES GET RESULTS

SECTION 1

JOB-GETTING RESUMES

SECTION 2

GETTING READY TO WRITE YOUR RESUME

SECTION 3

WRITING THE RESUME

SECTION 4

THE COVERING LETTER

APPENDIX

INTRODUCTION

RESUMES GET RESULTS

YOU NEED A RESUME

The resume gets you the job you are after. The resume summarizes employable you at a glance. When the resume is prepared properly, wheels turn faster and doors open oftener. With the right resume, each step in your job campaign is more productive. When the resume is slapped together or canned, responses dwindle.

It is inconceivable that any job applicant in administration, business, or the professions would campaign without a resume. Moreover, today's personnel trends favor the applicant with a resume, in all areas, on all levels, for all kinds of jobs—artisan, industrial, skilled trades, part time, or temporary.

The business executive, engineer, foreman, physician, secretary, or teacher seeking employment is expected to enclose a resume with the covering letter and to carry a resume into the interview. The bank guard, camp counselor, machinist, photographer, or waitress who offers an attractive, appropriate resume will impress the employer as a superior job candidate.

This book provides valuable tips to guide you in building the right resume *for you*. All the resumes in Section 1 of this book are structured on resume-building tips that appear throughout this book.

EMPLOYABLE YOU AT A GLANCE

The word *resume* (from the French *résumé*) means *summary*. Although some persons still retain the French spelling with two accent marks and the French pronunciation *ray-zu*-MAY, most personnel people prefer the streamlined spelling *resume* and the English pronunciation REZ-*uh-may*.

All resumes summarize; they present *essential information* in the briefest language possible. All resumes *tabulate* data, that is, they present information in a form that resembles a *data table*. Compare the diagrams on page 2 and you will see how the *tabulated data* of the resume differs from the usual page of written prose.

1

Tabulated Data on a
Resume Page

Paragraphed Data on a
Prose Page

Note how the data on the resume page is grouped for reading *at a glance*. Headings, indentions, brief entries, and white space are used freely.

Contrast this tabulated page with the more usual paragraphing of sentences on the prose page (to the right above). The prose page is excellent for discussions in reports, letters, and books; but it is not the approach you need to profile your best self in the job campaign.

Now leaf through Section 1, "Job-Getting Resumes" (beginning on page 5). Note how many different forms the resume can take; yet note how all of these resumes are tabulated for action. Note how you respond instantly to some resumes as your kind of resume—*resume styles which look and sound like you*. Note how other resumes, though not your style, may be appropriate for some relative or acquaintance.

A resume is *right* when it is attractive, businesslike, professional, and appropriate. A resume is *appropriate* when it fits the occasion and does full justice to you. It must look like you, feel like you, and present the best image of you.

THE RESUME IN THE JOB CAMPAIGN

A good resume serves as a valuable tool at all steps in the job campaign.

The Occupational Worksheet. Early in the campaign, you analyze yourself in terms of job opportunity and develop a self-inventory called the OCCUPATIONAL WORKSHEET (See pages 124 and 179). The occupational worksheet affords a view of self that gives you the foundation for your resume.

The Job Market. You often move into the JOB MARKET. The job market has many different gateways, all highly important to you, but each one slightly different from the others. All of these gateways require RESUMES.

Some of the gateways have big invitations on them. These are the INVITED GATEWAYS; the prospective employer makes public the fact that he needs somebody like you in his organization. He runs WANT ADS in the newspapers or recruits at schools or through agencies.

Some of the gateways bear no special invitation, but these gateways do lead to highly desirable jobs. These are the UNINVITED GATEWAYS. As an applicant, you apply because you know that in all likelihood the prospective employer needs someone like you in his organization. You PROSPECT for a job the way an enterprising salesman prospects for sales.

Some of these gateways must be entered through letters—INVITED and UNINVITED LETTERS OF APPLICATION. Some of these gateways involve APPLICATION BLANKS and even TESTS. But all of these GATEWAYS require RESUMES.

The Interview. You can present a resume when a clerk or receptionist tries to offer you a preliminary (screening) application blank. Your resume shows you to advantage; a preliminary application blank may stress some defect that eliminates you without an interview.

Often you can present a resume as an advantageous icebreaker at the opening of an interview. And very often a personnel person will pattern the interview on your resume, a course most advantageous for you.

HOW THIS BOOK CAN HELP YOU GET A JOB

This book will help you shape a resume that defines you to best advantage in the job campaign. The resume is vital to your success at every step in getting the job that is right for you. As we noted, a solid resume is the passkey to many tightly locked doors in job campaigning. But, equally valuable, the process of preparing a resume pays dividends over and above the value of the resume as a door opener. This book provides many direct and indirect benefits in its four main sections and Appendix.

Section 1 presents 83 resumes showing display patterns, substance, and phrasing to guide you in composing the resume that suits you best. It is not enough that a resume be right; that resume must also be right for you. But Section 1 does much more. It gives you insight into jobs now available and the qualifications needed to fill those jobs.

Section 2 shows you how to gather material for the resume and how to organize that material in the occupational worksheet. But in a larger sense, Section 2 shows you how to evaluate yourself in terms of the job market, how to decide on turns in your career, and how to have available the right data for all aspects of career planning and job getting.

Section 3 explains the fundamentals of resume writing. It builds on principles of job getting, psychological and graphic perception, and effective phrasing. Section 3 specifies the fundamentals incorporated in the guide resumes in Section 1. Again these insights extend to other aspects of the job campaign.

Section 4 explains and illustrates the composition of a covering letter. These insights tie into general campaigning, resume writing and interviewing. The views of invited and uninvited applications and the comments on special campaign letters demonstrate some of the principles of general campaign strategies.

The Appendix offers two occupational worksheet specimens. The grouping and interpretation of worksheet data display the fundamentals of organizing oneself for the job campaign. The occupational worksheet is a source for resume substance, but it is a source also for interview substance and campaign strategies. A good occupational worksheet organizes you for the job campaign and for your career.

SECTION 1

JOB-GETTING RESUMES

How can you make the most out of the guidance offered in this book? Very easily.

STEP 1. Consult the alphabetic list of occupations, professions, and work areas which begins on the next page. Find the job title or job area that interests you. If you cannot find the precise title you want, settle for the area closest to the one you want to target.

STEP 2. Turn to the page or pages indicated next to the title. Consider the resume you find as a model or guide for composing your own resume. Use that resume as a guide or model if it feels right for you; substitute your details for those found in the resume.

STEP 3. Glance through all the other resumes displayed in this section, "Job-Getting Resumes." Consider any other resume that feels right for you as a possible model or guide for composing your own resume. Use any other resume as a guide or model, even if it is not in your area, but substitute your details for those in the guide resume.

For fully detailed, illustrated guidance on career selection and organizing details, consult Section 2, "Getting Ready to Write Your Resume." For specific help with resume display and phrasing, consult Section 3, "Writing the Resume." For how-to-do-it instructions on writing the covering letter consult Section 4, "The Covering Letter." Whenever you have any question at any step, consult the index to locate the illustrated help you need. For general information on careers, jobs, and corporations, consult the job-reference books listed in the Appendix.

8

PETER A. TRIPELER

    414 Parkview Drive   M A N A G E M E N T
    Rye, New York 98765
    (345) 765 9078   A C C O U N T A N T

    Married, 2 children; excellent health; 5'8"; 165 pounds; 27 years
    old

    CAREER OBJECTIVE: To join a major corporation as management
    accountant and become controller or treasurer in time.

Education

Bachelor of Science, Accounting, College of Business and Public
 Administration, New York University, 1975-1978. Attended college
 evenings while working full time in Controller's department of
 Sennico Oil Company and Rectivox Electronics. (See below)

Advanced Accounting Courses	Business Background Courses
Management Accounting	Advanced Topics in Financial
Accounting for Decision	Corporate Management
Making and Control	Industrial and Managerial
Computer-Based Information	Economics
Systems	Management Information Systems
Advanced Federal Tax Laws	Quantitative Analysis of
Seminar in Management	Business Operations
Accounting	Business Communication

Experience

Junior Accountant, Sennico Oil Company, New York, N.Y., 1978-Present.
 Worked on various assignments in the Controller's office using IBM
 ledger system. This work related to sophisticated computer accounting
 training at New York University and made it possible for me to
 accept accelerated responsibility. Desire change because my degree
 qualifies me for advanced responsibility not possible in present
 position structure. I have discussed this decision thoroughly with
 Controller, who wants me to stay with Sennico until I get a new post.

Accounting Clerk, Rectivox Electronics, New York, N.Y., 1973-1978.
 Full-charge and general ledger bookkeeping. Worked with IBM ledger
 system, prepared financial statements, and rotated as back-up
 accounting clerk as needed.

Military Experience

United States Army, 1969-1971, Sergeant Infantry, Vietnam, wounded in
 action, Silver Star, no disability.

References

Full references will be supplied on request.

11

ADMINISTRATIVE ASSISTANT

PATRICIA MCMAHON

150 Wallingford Boulevard   administrative
Houston, Texas 09876
(123) 456 7890   assistant
    Single; excellent health; 5'4", 115 pounds; 26 years old

──────────────── OBJECTIVE ────────────────

        To serve a hard-working executive who needs an
        assistant with enterprise and the capacity to take
        over routine functions and detailed work.

──────────────── EXPERIENCE ────────────────

Plastic Porcelain Company   Wyeth, Texas

    Administrative Assistant, January 1977 to Present
        Confer with Plant Superintendent daily, reviewing day's work.
        Help develop daily work schedule.
        Supervise head office clerical force, eliminate backlogs.
        Review inventory and allied records.
        Maintain Plant Superintendent's office.
        Troubleshoot as typist, bookkeeper, record clerk.

Houston Electronic Industries   Houston, Texas

    Gal Friday, April 1972 to January 1977
        Started as secretary but assumed all office responsibility.
        Reported to proprietor daily on all office procedures.
        Kept all books and all records; prepared payroll.
        Resolved administrative problems in absence of proprietor.
        Assisted customers who called on telephone or in person.

──────────────── EDUCATION ────────────────

Southwest School of Business   Houston, Texas

    Certificate in Business Skills, February 1976 to January 1977
        Qualified in bookkeeping, typing, shorthand, and dictaphone.
        Qualified in basic office computing machines.
        Qualified in machine records.

Houston Commercial High School   Houston, Texas

    Commercial Course Diploma, February 1968 to February 1972

──────────────── REFERENCES ────────────────

Present employer knows of my intention to take new position. Specific
references will be furnished on request.

J O H N T. M A X W E L L

345 Tighe Street
Palz, Ohio 23456   a d v e r t i s i n g   m a n a g e r
(234) 567 8902

Objective   To provide a large manufacturing, wholesaling,
             or retailing corporation with creative,
             imaginative, sales-building advertising programs

All-Points Advertising and Promotion Experience

Advertising Manager, Greenville Insurance Company, Greenville, Ohio,
   1973-present. This $40,000,000 company sponsors an automobile club
   in the states of Ohio, Indiana, Illinois, and Michigan, providing
   accident insurance and free towing service. It has recently entered
   the life insurance field under the subsidiary Scioto Life Insurance.
   My duties consist of:

   ● planning all advertising and promotion campaigns in
     consultation with president and sales manager;

   ● conducting all newspaper, billboard, and direct mail
     advertising on a budget of $200,000;

   ● managing a staff of ten, including one artist and one
     copywriter; and

   ● guiding the new Hoosier-Wabash subsidiary in its first year
     of development, designing promotional programs with stock
     options for brokers and agents.

Since coming to this firm in 1973 sales have increased 200%. Tests
show that my promotions draw sales of 5 to 8%. Desire to change
because I am ready for wider, higher-echelon responsibility.

Advertising Manager, Bremerton Department Stores, New York City;
   Garden City, Long Island; Paramus, New Jersey, 1967-1973. This
   discount-type general department store chain grosses $75,000,000 a
   year. As advertising manager I made daily, Sunday, holiday, and
   special-event layouts for newspaper ads and supervised preparation
   of copy and production; I supervised the production of radio and TV
   announcements. I prepared all stuffers for continuous campaign
   mailings to charge customers. Left to gain higher responsibility at
   Greenville Insurance.

Copywriter, Perkins, Dietz, and Holladay Agency, New York City,
   1965-1967. This agency had billings of $2,000,000 in the grocery
   food market. I wrote all copy for Baby's Own infant foods, the
   agency's largest account. Left for position of greater managerial
   responsibility at Bremerton.

Professional Training in Advertising and Sales

Certificate in Direct Mail Advertising. Academy of Direct Mail
    Advertising League of New York, 1968. While working for Bremerton
    Department Stores, I took an eight-week course and seminar in direct
    mail advertising. My model letters won first prize and earned me an
    $800 award.

Certificate in Sales Promotion. School of Continuing Education, New
    York University, 1969. While working for Bremerton, I completed
    three advanced courses in sales, sales promotion, and advertising
    which led to a special certificate. These courses were conducted by
    leading authorities in all three fields.

Bachelor of Science, Marketing. St. John's University, Queens, New
    York, 1964. Trained in all phases of marketing, with heavy emphasis
    in advertising and sales.

Personal Data

Born September 21, 1942, in Brooklyn, New York; parents owned a small
    neighborhood department store where I worked part time and summers
    during high school and college. Both parents still living.

Married with two sons and a daughter. Own my home in Palz, free and
    clear. Finances in excellent condition; no debts.

Excellent health; passed physical examination in May for purchase of
    $10,000 policy with Scioto Life Insurance Company.

References

Mr. Matthew LaPlante, President, Greenville Insurance Company,
    Greenville, Ohio.

Mr. David Macaleavy, Vice President, Bremerton Department Stores,
    Garden State Plaza, Paramus, New Jersey.

Mr. Alvin Hamlett, Advertising Manager, Baby's Own, Inc., 654
    Lexington Avenue, New York City.

Mr. Murray Neill, Jr., Executive Secretary, Direct Mail Advertising
    League of New York, 876 Madison Avenue, New York City.

AIRLINE RESERVATIONIST

MARY MCCARTHY

Trained and Experienced
Airline Reservationist

65 Jefferson Avenue
Utica, New York 09876
(123) 456 7890

Single, good appearance
5'8", 135 pounds
26 years old, healthy

OBJECTIVE: To serve large commercial airline as senior or
supervising reservationist, with continuing contributions
that would earn advancement to managerial position in
operating division.

Airline Experience

RESERVATIONIST, Delaware and Hudson Airways, Inc., Utica, N.Y.
January 1975 to Present.

Perform all duties at airport office: make reservations for
flights to points in Middle Atlantic States; arrange connecting
flights; type and teletype; and operate small computer. Desire
position with larger carrier.

GROUND HOSTESS, Prairie State Airways, Chicago, Illinois. June
1973 to January 1975.

Assisted passengers in line at reservation desk or waiting to
board planes at O'Hare Airport.

Professional Training

CERTIFICATE, Airways and Travel Vocational School, June 1973.

Completed sixteen-week course in travel-office management, with
emphasis on computer and clerical procedures.

COMMERCIAL DIPLOMA, Rochester High School, Rochester, N.Y.,
February 1973.

Trained in office machines, bookkeeping, and social business
subjects, along with general high school courses.

Main Interests

Hiking in mountainous regions, reading, and travel.

References

Full references will be furnished on request. My present
employer knows of my desire to change positions. You may
contact Delaware and Hudson Airways.

15

ARCHITECT

JAMES T. ATHENAKIS

20 Wilbur Way
Parsons, Vermont 09876
(123) 456 7890

A R C H I T E C T

Born: May 1, 1938
Marital Status: Married, six sons
Height: Six feet
Weight: 190 pounds
Health: Excellent

OBJECTIVE

To associate with national architectural firm specializing in the design and construction of commercial buildings that fit ethos of the community.

EXPERIENCE

Supervising Architect, Green Lakes Corporation, Boston Massachusetts, 1970 to Present. Builders of multistory office buildings, primarily for banks, savings and loan associations, and public utilities.

Confer with clients in all parts of continental United States, Puerto Rico, Alaska, and Hawaii and with municipal planning boards and recommend designs that meet requirements of clients, planners, zoning laws, and building codes; develop final plans with assistance of planning architects and staff engineers; and oversee construction through staff of five assisting architects.

Staff Architect, Travers Construction Company, Cleveland, Ohio, 1965-1970. Builders of supermarkets, housing projects, and commercial buildings.

Served as liaison architect between Travers management and firms of designing architects and consulting engineers, translating ideas of clients, officials, company management, and engineers into feasible design. Considerable planning and replanning of interior details, but main emphasis on exterior design.

EDUCATION

Bachelor of Architecture (five-year program), School of Architecture, Green Mountain University, Montpelier, Vermont, 1956-1961.

MILITARY

Architect, Corps of Engineers, U.S. Army (Captain), 1961-1963. Trained in structural engineering and military building design. Commended (Legion of Merit, Chevalier) for design of officers' club which has been widely adopted at army posts in United States.

REFERENCES

References will be furnished on request.

allen p. kalbfleisch   A R T

_____D I R E C T O R

           forty-five regent street
           marblehill, n.y. 98765
           (456) 890 4567

       objective | to supervise art department in advertising agency,
                     | magazine, or book publisher

            art | ART DIRECTOR, EBER & HART, monticello, ohio,
       experience | advertising agency, bookings at $8,000,000. full
                     | charge of all visualization, layout, and development
          1970- | of magazine displays; manage department, preparing
         present | budget, purchasing supplies, hiring and evaluating
                     | personnel, and representing department in all agency
                     | conferences; supervise all art production; and design
                     | and execute unusual displays. have apartment in new
                     | york city area and want to join new york firm.

          1965- | MANAGER OF ART DEPARTMENT, PRESCOTT BOOKS, columbus,
          1970 | ohio, publishers of children's books, trade and text,
                     | sold in department stores and bookstores, with
                     | textbook adoptions in forty-five states. supervised
                     | the work of staff assistant and ten artists; worked
                     | closely with publisher, editors, and authors in design
                     | of all books; reconciled all art concepts with budget
                     | and production costs; supervised all routine designs;
                     | supervised and assisted artists in drawing and
                     | illustrations; and worked directly with printers in
                     | all phases of production. left Prescott for wider
                     | experience offered by Eber & Hart.

          1963- | STAFF ARTIST, HOME AND FAMILY MAGAZINE, cleveland,
          1965 | ohio, national magazine sold in supermarkets and chain
                     | grocery stores. responsible for all layouts, photo
                     | displays, and original drawings. worked directly with
                     | editor-in-chief and printers. advised and assisted
                     | advertisers and writers.

            art | COMMERCIAL ART INSTITUTE OF NEW YORK, new york city.
        education | advanced training in all phases of commercial art
                     | including visualization, layout, typography, lettering,
          1961- | sketching, cartooning, and production. studied under
          1963 | teaching fellowship. awarded five prizes for
                     | advertisements.

          1957- | BACHELOR OF FINE ARTS (BFA) DEGREE, SCIOTO INSTITUTE,
          1961 | columbus, ohio. basic training in all media--oil
                     | painting, wash drawings, line drawings, cartooning.
                     | won five prizes. studied under full scholarship.

        personal | born june first, nineteen-thirty-five; single; healthy

       references | complete references on request

ARTHUR C. BANNISTER   BANK ATTORNEY

234 Palisades Avenue, Mont Rosa, Oregon 23456; (687) 234-5678

Objective	To serve in the legal department, personal trust department, or corporate trust department of a bank in a large city.
Education	J.D. degree, New York University, 1979 (evenings). Member of Bar, State of Oregon, 1980.
	B.S. degree, Oregon State University, 1975. Major in economics with minor banking; earned tuition and maintenance by typing for Legal Department of Third National Bank of Salem in the evenings.
Experience	Assistant Trust Officer, Broadway National Bank, Mont Rosa, Oregon, August 1979 to present.

Main Duties: Interview persons requesting personal trust information; design personal trusts, administer trusts, and speak to community groups.

Reason for Wanting Change: Desire position with a bank in a larger city.

Assistant Manager, Metropolitan Bank and Trust Company, New York City, 1975-1979.

Main Duties: Hired as economic analyst in Investment Review Section of Personal Trust Department. Transferred as assistant manager to Corporate Trust Department. Transferred as contract review manager to Legal Department in 1977.

Reason for Leaving: Returned to Oregon to study for state bar examination.

Typist, Third National Bank of Salem, Legal Department, 1971-1975 (evenings).

Personal	27 years old; single with no dependents; 5'9"; 160 pounds; excellent health.
References	Full references will be furnished on request.

AUDITOR

Clark C. Mallory

567 Main Street
Shenandoah,
Oregon, 98765
(345) 576 8967

OBJECTIVE
TO SERVE MAJOR INDUSTRIAL CORPORATION
AS FINANCIAL-TECHNICAL AUDIT MANAGER

42 years old; single; 5'6", 152 pounds; excellent health; enjoy travel.

EXPERIENCE AS OPERATIONAL AUDITOR

Fifteen years of heavy operational auditing experience with major
chemical products manufacturer and large power and gas public
utility, after thorough training in engineering (BSEE) and
accounting (MBA).

AUDIT   Nine years' experience with Thales Chemical, Inc. as
MANAGER Operational Auditor 1969-1973 and Audit Manager (1973-Present).
         I designed the basic systems and procedures for enlarging the
financial audit of this company to a full audit that included engineering
design, production, and control.

My system integrated perfectly with the financial audit and qualified me
for the top audit post when incumbent Audit Manager retired. Responsible
for both the financial and production audit of the company and reported
directly to the President.

INTERNAL Six years' experience with Metropolitan Utility as Internal
AUDITOR   Auditor (1963-1969). I reviewed all accounts, contracts,
          disbursements, and field performance of contract analysts
(vegetation, gas, and wiring). My unique combination of engineering and
accounting made possible my writing procedures for this type audit and the
resultant report. These procedures are still used by this utility.

EDUCATION

Master of Business Administration (MBA), Graduate School of Business
   Administration, New York University, 1963.

Bachelor of Science, Electrical Engineering (BSEE), Lycurgus
   Technical Institute, Lycurgus, New York, 1960.

MILITARY

First Lieutenant, United States Army, Signal Corps, Instructor in
   Electronics, Fort Monmouth, 1960-1962.

REFERENCES

Complete references will be supplied on request.

BANK TELLER

JOAN P. RODRIGUEZ

456 Maine Street   Born April 5, 1959
Leeds, Iowa 98765   5'6", 126 pounds
(345) 889 8765   Single

Objective   To work as bank teller

Education   Graduate of Leeds High School, Commercial Course,
               June 1978.

               Commercial Courses   Background Courses

               Bookkeeping   English
               Business Machines   Economics
               Business Mathematics   Civics
               Business Law   History
               Stenography   Economic History

Activities   Treasurer of Student Council, 1979-1980

               Treasurer of Junior Class, 1978

               President of Civics Club, 1977

Experience   Clerk-Typist, First National Bank of Leeds, Bay Avenue
               Branch, Summer 1979.

               Cashier, Shop-Quik Supermarket, Leeds, summers and
               Saturdays, 1977-1979.

Hobbies   Sewing and knitting. Awarded prizes at County Fair
               1979 and at State Fair 1978 for needlework.

References   Mr. Anthony T. LaGrange, Manager, Bay Avenue Branch,
               First National Bank of Leeds

               Mr. Alvin Marshall, Chairman, Commercial Studies
               Department, Leeds High School

               Miss Sylvia Lynch, Bookkeeping and Business Machines
               Instructor, Leeds High School.

BENEFITS AND COMPENSATION MANAGER

<u>EVELYN TROTTA</u>

7570 Remington Street
Brooklyn, N.Y. 11229
(212) 646-0987

Excellent Health
27 years old
Married

<u>OBJECTIVE</u>   To manage the employee benefits section of a corporate
            personnel department; plan and develop all compensation
programs; administer salary policies; procure insurance coverage for
groups and major medical; and earn advancement to personnel generalist
executive position.

<u>EXPERIENCE</u>   Five years heavy benefits and compensation experience with
multidivision corporation and with international management consulting
firm specializing in employee benefits, compensation, and job structure.

- <u>Benefits and Compensation Administrator</u>, TIGHE, WATTERS,
  AND BAILEY, INC., New York City, (1977-present). Manage
  corporate compensation section of this $3 billion mining
  corporation. Design, develop, implement, and review all
  benefits and compensation programs through staff of 25
  analysts and clerks. Interact with top management,
  personnel officers, and employees. Negotiate with carriers.
  Survey job and salary structures and innovate bonus,
  executive compensation, and other incentive systems.

- <u>Consulting Analyst</u>, BROUNARD AND LINK, Insurance
  Consultants and Brokers, New York City (1975-1977).
  Consulted with top-echelon officers and with personnel
  departments of large corporations. Reviewed current
  programs, innovated and revised both compensation and
  benefit programs. Obtained special packages for carriers.
  Wrote proposals and reports and made oral presentations
  to both management and employee groups.

<u>EDUCATION</u>   Professionally trained in college, insurance institute,
            and personnel programs. Have passed two actuarial tests
and now scheduled for third test.

- <u>Certificates</u>, AMERICAN INSTITUTE OF INSURANCE (1975);
  AMERICAN INSTITUTE OF PERSONNEL EXECUTIVES (1977).

- <u>Bachelor of Science</u>, RUTGERS UNIVERSITY, Newark, Major:
  Finance (June 1974).

<u>MEMBERSHIP</u>   American Compensation Association; National Personnel
            Association; Compensation and Benefits Association of New
            York; American Businesswomen's Association; Beta Gamma
Sigma, a national scholastic honor fraternity for collegiate schools of
business.

BIOCHEMIST

ANN M. FOX

24 Kenny Drive   Date of Birth: Feb. 7, 1952
North Orange, N.J. 07988   Height, Weight: 5'10", 140 lbs.
201/377-9876   Health: Excellent

OBJECTIVE

Position as biochemistry research aide

EXPERIENCE

Two years' experience at Georgetown University, Washington, D.C.
  June, 1978 to present

DUTIES

Organizing experiments   Full charge of scheduling and planning
                            experiments; setting up and dismantling
                            of equipment; and coordinating research
                            with other laboratory activities.

Dissecting specimens   Responsibility for all routine
                            dissections and for conduct of toxicity
                            tests.

Maintaining manual   Full charge of laboratory manual,
                            including manual custody and accuracy
                            of all entries made by staff.

One year's experience as biology teacher at Foxhill High School,
  Bloomside, N.J. September, 1977 to June, 1978. Taught additional
  courses in chemistry and general science.

EDUCATION

Master of Science in biology, University of Chicago, June, 1977,
  concentrated in biochemistry.

Bachelor of Science in biology with a minor in chemistry, University
  of Pittsburgh, June, 1975.

HONORS AND AWARDS

Ecology Essay Award by the Professional Women's Environmental
  Association of Illinois.

Phi Beta Kappa, University of Pittsburgh.

REFERENCES

References will be furnished upon request.

BOOKKEEPER

DANIEL HAVERMAN

863 Glenside Road
Camden, New Jersey 09876
(123) 456 7890

FULL-CHARGE BOOKKEEPER FIVE YEARS' EXPERIENCE

Experience

May, 1976- Present	**Talcott Curtain Company, Philadelphia** Handle complete set of books, cash disbursement, cash receipts, payroll, sales register, general ledger postings, and summarizations. Supervise two assistant bookkeepers. Company moving to New York City in September.
June, 1973- May, 1976	**Camden Food Industries, Camden** Handled cash reconciliation, bank reconciliations, subledgers, and general ledger postings. Began as assistant but promoted to full charge.

Education

Evenings June, 1971- June, 1974	**Philadelphia College of Business** Thorough training in accounting and bookkeeping leading to diploma. Program included:

Accounting 1 .... Foundations
Accounting 2 .... Proprietorships
Accounting 3 .... Partnerships
Accounting 4 .... Corporations
Accounting 5 .... Computers
Accounting 6 .... Taxes
Accounting 7 .... Payrolls

1969-1973	**Camden Commercial High School** Commercial diploma. Courses covered bookkeeping, typing, office practice, commercial arithmetic, and correspondence.

Personal

Born May 7, 1952
Single
Excellent health
5'7", 160 pounds

BUYER

m i l d r e d   g e o r g e

234 stedman parkway
south orange
new jersey 09003
(201) 234 7654

BUYER OF

LADIES' SHOES

job goal
: to serve as buyer of ladies' shoes for large retail organization grossing one million dollars annual sales in ladies' shoes.

present position
: ladies' shoe buyer, QUALITY DEPARTMENT STORE, englewood, new jersey. 1973-present.

- complete charge of ladies' shoe department . . . annual ladies' shoe sales, $250,000 . . . supervise five full-time and three part-time sales assistants.

- study preferences of customers in north jersey through field research and review of merchandise demands.

- purchase all ladies' shoes through visits to markets and through reception of manufacturers' representatives.

- check, verify, and authorize payment of all invoices.

previous position
: assistant buyer, ladies' shoes, BOSTON DEPARTMENT STORE, boston, massachusetts. 1969-1973.

- hired by this major department store ($850,000 ladies' shoe sales) as assistant buyer while senior at boston state university.

- learned the operation of ladies' shoe department thoroughly, starting with the physical checking and verifying of merchandise, the coding of tags and records, and the preparation of advertising and publicity.

- purchased merchandise on my own responsibility in the field and in the store; eight very successful assistant buyers' sales.

education
: bachelor of science in marketing, BOSTON STATE UNIVERSITY, 1971. earned tuition working as sales clerk in shoe store and as assistant buyer, boston department store.

personal
: 29 years old, single, 5'2", 110 pounds, excellent health.

references
: Full references on request.

24

CAMP COUNSELOR

ROGER P. MACFADDEN
Camp Counselor

College Address (To May 25)
456 Western Dormitory
Buchanan College
Buchanan, Massachusetts
(134) 345 5678

Home Address (Messages Forwarded)
78 Roseland Avenue
Cranford, Massachusetts
(134) 456 7890

PERSONAL   21 years old; excellent health; athletic;
             6'2", 195 pounds; very good appearance.

OBJECTIVE   To serve as head counselor or senior counselor
             of top-flight camp for boys 7 to 17.

EXPERIENCE AS CAMP COUNSELOR

Athletic Counselor   Sa-Ra-Nac Camp, Fort Adirondack, New York.
                       Full charge of all sports, including swimming,
       1979   baseball, basketball, tennis, archery, and
                       riding. Supervised three junior counselors.
                       Scheduled all athletic events. Coached in all
                       sports.

Waterfront Counselor   Lake Flower Camp, Lake Flower, Maine.
                       Supervised all lake sports including swimming,
       1978   canoeing, sailing, and water polo. Full Red
                       Cross training and qualification.

Counselor   Bandigot Camp, Bandigot Island, Maine.
                       Supervised 100 boys. Adviser to camp
       1977   newspaper. Instructor in swimming,
                       basketball, and tennis.

PARTICIPATION IN CAMP PROGRAMS

Ten summers of participation in top-flight camps during childhood
and adolescence, including Pennecott, Teck-No-Sun, and Bandigot
Camps. Earned expert badges in all camp activities.   Represented
Pennecott in International Jamboree in 1969.

EDUCATION

Senior at Buchanan College, major history and minor in health
education. Hold varsity letters in baseball, basketball, swimming,
and track. Captain of basketball team. President of student
council. On honor roll every term.

REFERENCES

Professor Alvin Jaurus, Director of Athletics, Buchanan College.

Mr. Thomas Hornstein, Owner of Camp Sa-Ra-Nac, Fort Adirondack.

Mr. Stanley Witowski, Owner of Lake Flower Camp, Lake Flower.

CASHIER

MARGARET F. BURLEIGH
848 Ninth Avenue
Belmont, Oregon 97548
754 8897

Born April 8, 1932
5'8", 145 pounds
Excellent health
Married; 2 sons, 17, 19

OBJECTIVE   To work as full-time cashier in supermarket, retail store, or restaurant now that children are grown.

EXPERIENCE

1971-
present

Part-Time Cashier, Belmont Supermarket, Belmont, Oregon. Operated cash register at checkout counter. Worked 25 hours a week.

1953-
1956

Cashier, Leonard's Department Store, Spokane. Received payments in person and by mail; prepared monthly statement; and assisted bookkeeper.

1951-
1953

Accounts Receivable Clerk, Pioneer-Ford Wholesalers, Spokane. Received payments at counter or in mail, issued receipts, and recorded cash. Prepared and mailed bills monthly.

EDUCATION

1950

Belmont Business School, Belmont, Oregon. Six months' course in comptometry and other business machines.

1946-
1950

Belmont High School, Belmont, Oregon. Commercial Course.

REFERENCES

Mr. Paul Murray, vice-president, Pioneer-Ford Wholesalers, Spokane.

Mr. Charles J. Ripley, office manager, Leonard's Department Store, Spokane.

Mr. Harold Esterly, store manager, Belmont Supermarket, Belmont, Oregon.

CHEMIST

AGARWALA PANDIT

45 Stickney Drive
Valhalla, N. Y. 98765
(914) 445-9876

I N D U S T R I A L

C H E M I S T

U.S. Citizen	5'3", 115 lbs.	27 years old
Single	Excellent Health	Will travel

————EXPERIENCE————

Manager, Organic Chemistry, LUBIAR PHARMACEUTICAL COMPANY, Caxton, New York, (1977-Present)

Administer department of 25 chemists. Design, develop, and evaluate new drugs. Plan and organize new research programs. Integrate scale-up and process development. Interrelate with biological, clinical, pharmacy, and research and development areas.

Senior Chemist, INTERAMERICA CHEMICAL SOLVENTS, INC., Detroit, Michigan, (1976-1977)

Managed formula control laboratory; conducted all tests for quality control; interrelated with group leaders in production. Promoted from chemist in biological section, synthesized organic compounds and evaluated effects.

————EDUCATION————

Master of Science, Physical and Organic Chemistry, GRADUATE SCHOOL OF ARTS AND SCIENCES, NEW YORK UNIVERSITY, (1975-1976).

Tuition and expenses paid from earnings and tuition remission as laboratory assistant. Average 3.7/4.0.

Bachelor of Science, Chemistry. POLYTECHNIC INSTITUTE OF BROOKLYN, N.Y., (1971-1975).

Fully trained in all basics of chemistry. Transferred 30 credits in mathematics from University of Punjab, making it possible to take graduate-level courses in mathematics and physical chemistry. Earned tuition by working evenings in a large drugstore.

————BACKGROUND————

Born in India. Visited United States in 1970, toured universities and chemical manufacturers. Moved to the United States in 1971. U.S. citizenship was granted in 1976. Full references will be supplied on request.

CLERK-TYPIST

WORK EXPERIENCE, SKILL TRAINING, AND EFFICIENCY RECORD

OF HELEN D'ARCY, CLERK-TYPIST

<u>Address</u>   <u>Personal</u>

419 Hagarstown Road   24 years old, single
Granville, Ohio 23456   5'7", 125 pounds
  (234) 567 8902   Excellent health

      JOB OBJECTIVE: To provide efficient, high-quality
      typing and clerical service to a business firm
      in the Columbus, Ohio, area.

<u>EXPERIENCE</u>

June 1978- <u>Rasmussen and Crandall, Insurance Brokers,</u> 210 State St.,
Present   Columbus, Ohio.

           Typed revised reports, assembled data from records and
           filled in various forms, filed records, served as desk
           receptionist, and provided general office assistance.

           Have given notice to Mr. Jay Rasmussen. Desire job with
           more typing and more responsibility.

June 1975- <u>Derek and Wilson, Real Estate Brokers,</u> 43 Kenyon Drive,
June 1978   Mount Vernon, Ohio.

           Typed forms, filed records, served as desk receptionist,
           and provided general assistance.

           Accepted job offer to work in Columbus from Rasmussen and
           Crandall.

<u>EDUCATION</u>   Graduate, Commercial Diploma, June 1975, Newark High
           School, Newark, Ohio, with the following business skills
           courses:
                 Typing, 3 years .... 70 wpm
                 Office Practice, 1 year ..... proficient
                 Business Machines, 1 year ... orientation
                 Shorthand, 2 years .... 115 wpm

<u>HOBBIES</u>   Bowling and tennis.

<u>REFERENCES</u>   Mr. Jay Rasmussen, Partner, Rasmussen and Crandall.

           Mr. Daniel Wilson, Partner, Derek and Wilson.

           Mr. Calvin Berkeley, Teacher of Business Subjects,
           Newark High School, Newark, Ohio.

ALBERT T. SWATHMORE
98 Salina Street
Syracuse, N.Y. 87654
(234) 456 7890

HOUSE ORGAN EDITOR
30 years old
5'10", 190 pounds
Single

objective   To serve as a house organ editor or technical editor
             with a manufacturer of electronic equipment or with a
             technical journal in any area of mechanics

experience   Three years' experience as publications editor with
             electronic manufacturers and a trade journal

1979-   ULTRASONIC INSTRUMENT, INC., AUBURN, NEW YORK, manager of
present   presentations. Full charge of all written publications,
             including company newsletter, magazine, proposals,
             reports, manuals, and scientific articles prepared
             by engineers and physicists. Direct a staff of 25 editors,
             writers, and typists. Many proposals cost $18,000 to
             $20,000 to produce, and many contracts involve expenditures
             in seven figures. Write and edit documents that range in
             language from highly technical to popular. Desire change
             because parent company, Stavanger, Inc., is selling
             Ultrasonic.

1978-   KASPAR CORDLESS INSTRUMENT COMPANY, UTICA, NEW YORK,
1979   technical writer. Wrote highly technical contract
             specifications, manuals, and articles requiring
             authoritative understanding of electronic design. My
             work attracted the interest of Ultrasonic management, a
             customer of Kaspar, leading to an offer to join Ultrasonic
             as manager of presentations.

1977-   ELECTRONICS ILLUSTRATED, NEW YORK CITY, feature writer.
1979   Reported new developments in both electronics and mechanics,
             interviewing scientists, studying models and blueprints,
             and corresponding with electronic specialists in all parts
             of the world.

education   Professional training in journalism and engineering

1977   Master of Science, Pulitzer School of Journalism, Columbia
             University

1975   Bachelor of Science, Electrical Engineering, New York
             University

references   Will be furnished on request

COMPUTER PROGRAMMER

Thomas Rivington
Computer Programmer
395 Park Avenue, Buffalo, New York 97503   Telephone (395) 598-7743

Personal

Born: February 7, 1955, in Ames, N.Y.   Health: Excellent
                                                Height: 6'1"
Marital Status: Single   Weight: 170 lbs.

Education

Dirksen University, Dirksen, N.Y.

Bachelor of Science, Mathematics, June 1977, in curriculum that
included:

Computer-Related Courses	Background Courses
Advanced computer science	Finite mathematics I & II
COBOL programming	Mathematical analysis
FORTRAN programming	Statistical analysis I & II
Systems design and analysis	Functions of compiled variables
Quantitative communication	Advanced systems management
Digital computer techniques	Technical report writing

Experience

Full-Time Experience

Systems Analyst, UM Electronics, Market Street, Utica, N.Y., 1977 to date.

        Flow-chart operations
        Devise gross systems designs
        Assist accountant in the use of computers
        Collect business information for management
        Solve problems electronically
        Update methods of operation

Part-Time and Summer Experience

Keypunch operator, Imperial Insurance Company, Utica, N.Y., June, 1976 to
September, 1976.

Stock clerk, Carl's Department Store, Utica, N.Y., June, 1975 to
September, 1975.

Extracurricular Activities

Varsity Track, 1974-1976
President, Mathematics Club

References

Prof. John D. Smith   Mr. Henry Gordon   Mr. Ralph McCrary
Chairman, Mathematics   Office Manager   Controller
Department   UM Systems   Imperial Insurance Co.
Dirksen University   7 Market Street   Utica, N.Y. 92754
Dirksen, N.Y. 92754   Utica, N.Y. 92754

30

COMPUTER SCIENCE REPRESENTATIVE

SYLVIA T. CLARKE

49 Salvestre Boulevard
Newark, Delaware 19711
(302) 123 4567

COMPUTER CUSTOMER SERVICE

REPRESENTATIVE

OBJECTIVE

To represent a computer management group, software designer,or
consultant, analyzing needs of prospective clients and
recommending software packages and tailored programs that solve
data-processing problems.

EXPERIENCE

Computer Customer Service Representative, KNIGHTSBRIDGE MANAGEMENT
GROUP, INC., Parr's Falls, Maryland. (1970-Present).

- Show presidents of universities and their systems analysts how to
  reduce operating costs by computerizing registration, grades,
  alumni records, printing labels, and payroll. Sell programs and
  services on the basis of these analyses and demonstrations.

- Assist designers and technicians in the implementation of new
  programs and supervise "walk-through" tests of newly installed
  systems.

- Orient all systems, technical support, and user groups to
  operation of newly installed systems. Demonstrate use of forms
  and edit forms to ensure clear keypunching and data processing.

- Survey university market for sales prospects.

- Schedule installations to insure completed deadlines and deploy
  work of designers and technicians.

- Train new Knightsbridge personnel in the field and in group
  classrooms. (Have trained twelve new field employees to date.)

EDUCATION

Bachelor of Arts, HOWARD UNIVERSITY, Washington, D.C., (1968-72).
Major: English, with 18 credits in business.

PERSONAL

Single; 30 years old; excellent health; 5'6", 125 lbs.

REFERENCES

Full references will be furnished on request.

MAIN-QUALIFICATION RESUME OF

CLARENCE C. MAGRUDERIN

Construction Foreman

45 Maxwell Drive
Ithaca, New York 09876
(345)234 8978

Heavy supervisory experience in both residential and
    commercial home building--ten years.

    Supervised the construction of all homes in three
    major New York State development tracts, working
    with architects and hiring building employees.

    Served as carpenter foreman for two large construction
    companies.

    Thoroughly trained in carpentry by master
    carpenters and U.S. Army Engineers.

Fully qualified as master carpenter with knowledge of all
    building trades. Skilled in layout. Trained draftsman.

Detailed resume will be sent on request.

A synopsis (qualification) resume is sent to screen
prospects. If response is gained, a fuller resume like one
on following page is sent to prospect. See discussion of
synopsis resume on pages 153-154.

CLARENCE C. MAGRUDERIN

Construction Foreman

Address and Telephone

45 Maxwell Drive
Ithaca, New York 09876
(345) 234 8978

Personal Details

35 years old
6'2", 201 pounds
Excellent health

OBJECTIVE   Supervisory position in residential or commercial
                 construction.

EXPERIENCE

1972-   Midstate Construction Company, Midstate, New York
Present
                 Project Foreman. Supervised the construction of all
                 the homes in the James Fenimore Cooper development.
                 Implemented all plans of architectural engineers.
                 Hired all employees. Oversaw and checked all work.
                 All Midstate contracts have been completed; need new
                 position.

1967-   Alhambra Construction Company, Alhambra, New York
1972
                 Master Carpenter and Construction Foreman. Joined
                 Alhambra as journeyman carpenter, but soon promoted to
                 master carpenter and placed in charge of carpenters
                 building and remodeling homes. I was responsible for
                 the work of twenty carpenters and apprentices.
                 Directed layout carpentry, installation of interior
                 and exterior carpentry, and flooring.

1964-   Selfridge Building and Supply, Ithaca, New York
1967
                 Apprentice and Journeyman Carpenter. Entered this
                 supply and building company as apprentice carpenter,
                 although I had qualified as a journeyman (equivalent)
                 in the U.S. Army. I assisted master carpenters on all
                 varieties of building and repairing both residential
                 and commercial structures. I learned purchasing and
                 estimating as sidelines.

MILITARY

1962-   U.S. Army, Sergeant, Engineering. My high aptitude in
1964   visual layout qualified me for specialized training in
                 construction. I achieved the equivalent of journeyman
                 carpenter. My leadership ability qualified me for the
                 position of project leader for erecting barracks in
                 continental United States and West Germany.

EDUCATION

June 1962	U.S. Army Engineering School, Fort Belvedere, Maryland Certificate in Carpentry
September– June 1961	Plaque Institute, Syracuse, New York Certificate in Drafting and Mechanical Design
1956– 1960	Eastwood High School, Syracuse, New York Scientific Course

SKILLS

Fully qualified in all phases of general carpentry. Thoroughly acquainted with lumber. Able to estimate construction costs for developing tracts. Adept in building layout and all surveying tools. Well acquainted with procedures of masonry, plumbing, electricity, heating, and landscaping.

REFERENCES

Mr. Alfred Keating, President, Midstate Construction Company, Midstate, New York

Mr. Thomas Mattingly, Vice President, Ithaca Central Savings and Loan Association, Ithaca, New York

Mr. Ralph Marington, Manager, Commercial Loan Department, Cincinnatus National Bank, Cincinnatus, New York

Mr. Perry Dragonette, President, Alhambra Construction Company, Alhambra, New York

SYNOPSIS RESUME OF ELIZABETH P. MEINICKE

Credit Manager

OBJECTIVE

To become credit manager of large manufacturing or wholesale
organization in Metropolitan New York area. Occupy important
credit manager post in Chicago, but desire to relocate in the
East for family reasons.

   Sixteen years of credit experience, thirteen years as
      credit manager.

- Now credit manager of large Chicago manufacturer
  with annual sales at $18,000,000 on open account.

- Previously credit manager of New Jersey
  manufacturer with sales of $6,000,000, and
  commercial loan supervisor with medium-sized bank.

  Master of Business Administration, finance, Graduate
      School of Business Administration, New York
      University.

  Bachelor of Science, accounting, School of Business,
      Seton Hall University, South Orange, New Jersey.

  Excellent health; married, two children; family life
      and finances in excellent condition.

Thirty-eight years old.

A synopsis (qualification) resume is mailed to screen
prospects. If response is gained, a fuller resume like
one on following page is sent to prospect. See discussion
of synopsis resume on pages 153-154.

ELIZABETH P. MEINICKE
Credit Manager

Address and Telephone   Personal Details

   45 Fort Dearborne Road   Born February 16, 1940
   Parkville Heights   5'6", 135 pounds
   Illinois 09876   Excellent health
   (244) 445 6789   Married, two children

SUMMARY

CREDIT AND COLLECTION MANAGER with sixteen years of heavy credit and
collections experience desires to relocate in the Metropolitan New York
area. Experience includes setting of credit policy, in collaboration
with controller and sales manager, and unrestricted authority in
carrying out this policy. Served two large manufacturers supplying both
wholesalers and dealers, extending credit and enforcing collections
through sophisticated and highly complicated credit and collection
systems. Also served in commercial credit department of a medium-sized
bank. Trained in finance and accounting, with Master of Business
Administration degree in finance, New York University, and Bachelor of
Science degree in accounting from Seton Hall University. Present
employer knows of this desire to relocate in New York area.

EXPERIENCE

Experience in Credit Management

CREDIT   Symplagades Adhesives, Inc., Chicago, one of the
MANAGER   nation's largest manufacturers of glues, pastes, and
1970-   other adhesives with annual sales of over eighteen
present   million dollars. Company distributes through 500
             wholesalers and jobbers, 3,500 dealers, and 13,000
tradesmen and mechanics. Sales involve five different forms of credit
accommodations, requiring exacting analysis procedures and collection
routines. Desire to relocate in New Jersey to be near family.

   Developed credit department from staff of five to present staff of
      twenty-seven. When hired, firm was a wholly owned subsidiary of
      California Primer and Sealer, distributing through CP&S with
      limited sales on open account. Symplagades separated from CP&S
      in 1971, making necessary the credit department I developed. All
      sales now open account.

   Established all credit and collection systems now in use, helped
      incorporate credit department as a module in total systems of
      Symplagades, dovetailing with billing and sales. Developed
      complicated interlocking sales intelligence, accounts receivable
      and collections systems.

Manage credit and collection staff, direct all credit analysis,
personally review all major accounts and readjust ratings,
personally approve large accommodations, and review
collections procedures periodically.

Serve as economic advisor to top management, production management,
and sales management.

CREDIT
MANAGER
1965-
1970

Fierenza Scents, Inc., Delawanna, New Jersey,
processor of essential oils and manufacturer of
perfumes and cosmetics, with sales at $6,000,000.
Working with this small, specialized chemical company
provided me with a thorough grounding in all phases of
credit and collections. With two assistants, I conducted all credit
analysis, approved all accommodations, and followed up all collections.
To enhance sales, my staff and I worked closely with marginal customers
and helped them through several difficulties. When this small company
was absorbed by Charleston Essential Oils, Inc., I accepted offer to
join Symplagades Adhesives.

Experience in Bank Credit

COMMERCIAL
LOAN
SUPERVISOR
1962-
1965

Bloomfield Trust Company, Bloomfield, New Jersey.
Upon graduation from Seton Hall, was engaged by this
$75,000,000 bank as a management cadet. After a
six months' orientation to all phases of banking,
was assigned to the commercial loan department.
Served as loan review supervisor and assistant on the
platform to the vice-president of commercial loans. This position
grounded me thoroughly in all phases of credit appraisal, the function
of the commercial bank in mobilizing the credit of a community, the
discounting of commercial papers, and the handling of insolvencies.

EDUCATION

Collegiate Training in Finance and Accounting

MASTER
OF BUSINESS
ADMINISTRATION
1965

Graduate School of Business Administration, New York
University. While working for Bloomfield Trust
Company, attended New York University evenings and
and summers to complete MBA degree in three years.
Specializing in finance, I had extensive training in
credit management under some of America's outstanding authorities on
these subjects.

BACHELOR
OF SCIENCE
1962

School of Business, Seton Hall University. Thoroughly
trained in accounting with minor in banking and
finance. Earned all of my tuition as an undergraduate
working for the State-Wide Credit Association. My

formal training coupled very nicely with my work in credit reporting.
Despite working evenings, I managed to serve as the business manager of
the undergraduate newspaper and the yearbook during my last two
semesters. Was awarded three prizes on graduation--Seth Boyden Award
for industrial management design, Kilduff Cup presented by American
Credit Report Association, and Women in Finance Plaque.

Special Training in Computer Systems

COMPUTER   While working for the Bloomfield Trust Company, I was
CERTIFICATES   sent to IBM Corporation at Endicott, New York, and
                Burroughs Corporation in New York City for special
computer training. These courses made it possible for me to assist in
the design and installation of computer systems at this bank.

IBM Certificate in "1401" Programming, awarded 1963.

Burroughs Corporation Certificate in "B-250" Programming, awarded
    in 1964.

REFERENCES

References covering all phases of experience will be furnished on
request.

DENTIST

<u>V I T A</u>

Albert T. Saffrian, D.D.S.
45 Park Place
Parksville, Illinois 09876
(123) 456 7890

Born May 1, 1948; excellent health; married, 2 sons; 5'9", 180 pounds

OBJECTIVE

To associate with an established dentist and possibly
form partnership, particularly interested in areas
lacking adequate dental service.

EXPERIENCE

<u>Staff Dentist,</u> Wabash Health Center, Chicago, Illinois,
1976-present. Heavy practice in all phases of general
dentistry including prosthetics. Outstanding experience
with top-flight facilities and professional associates,
but desire more personalized community practice and
patient relationship.

<u>Dental Officer</u> (Captain), United States Army, 1974-1976.
Heavy general practice in army dispensaries in Fort Dix
and Honolulu.

EDUCATION

<u>Doctor of Dental Surgery,</u> School of Dentistry,
Georgetown University, Washington, D.C., 1970-1974.

<u>Bachelor of Science</u> (Biology Major), Notre Dame University,
Notre Dame, Indiana, 1966-1970. Full extracurricular activity
including varsity football and presidency of senior class.

AWARDS

Phi Beta Kappa, Notre Dame University, 1970.

Georgetown General Dentistry Certificate, granted
for proficiency in clinical dental practice, 1974.

BACKGROUND

Born to pioneer Illinois family. Father a physician and
mother daughter of physician. Five brothers physicians.
Raised in Parksville and married to Parksville native.
Mrs. Saffrian has M.A. in Social Work (University of Chicago).

REFERENCES

Full references will be forwarded on request.

DIETITIAN

VITA

DOLORES JIMENEZ, R.D.

86 Maple Street   D I E T I T I A N
Troy, New York 09876
(345) 456 7890

Registered Dietitian, Excellent Health, Single, Will Relocate

---OBJECTIVE---

To serve as an administrative dietitian with a large hospital or as a
consultant with a dietetic consulting firm.

---EXPERIENCE---

Ten years' responsible experience as supervisory dietitian and as clinical
dietitian.

● Supervisory Dietitian, RAVENAL STATE HOSPITAL, Ravenal, New York
  (1974 to Present). Plan, tailor, assign, and review the work of three
  clinical dietitians. Serve as assistant director of food services in
  the management of kitchens and dining rooms. Plan and review programs
  for delivering special food needs of patients. Commended twice for
  work by Director of the Bureau of Nutrition Services, New York State
  Department of Mental Hospitals.

● Clinical Dietitian, PINE RIVER HOSPITAL, Pine River, Colorado (1972
  to 1974). Prepared all menus, managed kitchen and ambulatory dining
  facility. Assisted the hospital administrator in the planning and
  management of food services.

● Dietitian, STATE UNIVERSITY OF ROCKFORD, Rockford, Colorado (1970
  to 1972), while earning my M.S. degree in food science. Supervised
  kitchen and dining room, with full charge of all food services in
  400-student facility. Directed work of all kitchen personnel
  including two cooks.

---EDUCATION---

Full graduate and undergraduate training in food science, food management,
  and institutional management, including on-the-job training to qualify
  for Registered Dietitian examinations.

● Master of Science, STATE UNIVERSITY OF ROCKFORD, Rockford, Colorado
  (June 1972). Major: Food Science. Supportive program in anatomy,
  physiology, chemistry, biology, and institutional life.

● Bachelor of Science, RAWLINS INSTITUTE OF SCIENCE, Rawlins, Wyoming
  (June, 1969). Major: Food Science; Minor: Microbiology. After
  graduation, served six months' internship at PHYSICIANS HOSPITAL,
  Rawlins, Wyoming (1969). Passed all tests for membership in
  American Dietetic Association and Registered Dietitian certification.

PERCIVAL R. MESSMER

14 Marigold Terrace   D R A F T S M A N
Cherry Valley
New York 09876

OBJECTIVE: To serve as supervising draftsman with manufacturer
            of electrical or mechanical products.

EXPERIENCE

Supervising Draftsman, Sheffield Castings, Inc., Utica, New York,
1969 to present.

Hired as a senior draftsman to implement engineering designs of
pipes and fittings into working plans. Worked with both
cast-iron soil pipes and fiber sewer pipes. Introduced comments
on cost, durability, and feasibility for intended purpose. Given
increasing assistance of detailers, checkers, and tracers as
product line expanded and sales increased. Promoted to
supervising draftsman in charge of all pipes and pipe fittings
in 1971. Desire new position to expand my scope of supervision
and variety of products designed.

Senior Draftsman, Fairfield Fire Engines, Inc., Mohawk, New York,
1964-1969.

Hired as detailer to assist senior draftsman in designing basic
parts of mountings placed on truck chassis in building fire
engines. Promoted to senior draftsman when my superior retired,
and worked directly with engineer. Although firm small and
production time extended over many months, this position provided
invaluable training in gross and detailed design and in firsthand
work with both engineer and with craftsmen who custom build each
engine.

MILITARY

Sergeant, Corps of Engineers, U.S. Army, 1961-1964.

My training in drafting qualified me for assignment as draftsman
with 39th Engineer Group. While overseas, given training in
drafting of roads, bridges, and military fortification designs.
Remained in service six months longer when given opportunity to
take course in electronic drafting provided by Ordnance
Department.

EDUCATION

Certificate in Mechanical Drafting, Albany Technical School,
Albany, New York, 1960.

Graduate, Albany High School, 1959.

PERSONAL

Born May 5, 1942, single; 5'11"; 170 pounds; excellent health.

REFERENCES

Will be provided on request.

SYNOPSIS RESUME OF RAMSAY T. MARTIN

Economist

OBJECTIVE

Appointment to advisory and research post with government, business, industry, or conference board. Hold responsible position with major economic foundation, but desire more research responsibility and less administrative work.

Now chief economist with major economic
    foundation.

Two chairmanships on Presidential economic
    research committees.

Senior economist with one of nation's largest
    banks.

Experience as industrial economic consultant
    and instructor in economics.

Doctor of Philosophy in economics and Master
    of Arts in economics from Metropolitan
    University, New York.

Author, co-author, or editor of over two hundred
    articles, pamphlets, and studies of economic
    subjects.

Forty-eight years old; married; finances in
    excellent condition.

Health excellent.

A synopsis (qualification) resume is mailed to screen prospects. If response is gained, a fuller resume like one on following page is sent to prospect. See discussion of synopsis resume on pages 153-154.

RAMSAY T. MARTIN

Economist

14 Cosgrove Terrace, Rye, New York: (231) 456 7890

FINANCIAL AND INDUSTRIAL ECONOMIST with top-flight qualifications
available for appointment to advisory and research post with
government agency, business, industry, or conference board.
Qualifications include Doctor of Philosophy degree in economics,
chairmanship of two national study boards appointed by the
President of the United States, and posts as economist with
financial and manufacturing organizations.

EXPERIENCE

CHIEF ECONOMIST, FOUNDATION FOR AMERICAN ECONOMIC GROWTH, New York,
New York, 1972-present.

This privately funded research foundation has a staff of fifteen
full-time members and a consulting staff of twenty-five outstanding
economists. It issues a ten-page monthly report to business
leaders, government officials, and economists and ten to fifteen
pamphlets a year. These reports and pamphlets report and
interpret economic trends in terms comprehensible to businessmen,
government officials, teachers, community leaders and laymen.

As chief economist I participate as a full member of the Board of
Directors, work directly with funding groups in raising research
grants, design all research, supervise staff and consulting
economists, and analyze trends in government expenditures,
inflation, investments, labor, industrial growth, housing, and
community development.

As administrator I manage the foundation headquarters through a
chief clerk, editor, librarian, and statistician. I hire staff
personnel and engage research economists.

This work is interesting and challenging, but I would like an
appointment with more economic research and with less
administrative responsibility.

CHAIRMAN, PRESIDENTIAL COMMITTEE TO STUDY INFLATIONARY PRESSURES OF
INVESTMENT PROMOTION GROUPS, 1971-1972.

As chairman of this committee I supervised the work of five
research economists and seven clerical assistants in studying the
activities of one hundred organizations promoting private
investments and correlated these findings with available statistics
on inflation in areas directly and indirectly affected. This
analysis resulted in a five hundred-page report of narrative and
graphics needed by the Executive Division of the Federal Government.

43

CHAIRMAN, PRESIDENTIAL COMMITTEE TO STUDY CORRELATION OF INFLATION AND
MINORITY UNEMPLOYMENT IN NEW YORK, CHICAGO, AND LOS ANGELES, 1970-1971.

As chairman of this committee, I supervised and integrated the
research of three teams conducting studies in three metropolitan
areas. From my headquarters in Washington, D.C., with a small
office staff, I directed the research of regional teams and
joined various teams at critical points in the project. When
regional research was completed, I brought team leaders to
Washington where we compiled four important reports--an integrated
report and three regional reports.

SENIOR ECONOMIST, BANK OF THE PACIFIC, Los Angeles, California, 1965-1970.

Assisted by two staff economists and the research staff (when
needed) of the investment review section of the personal trust
division, I maintained constant surveillance over economic
environment of the bank, consulting with top management, issuing
reports, and conducting ad hoc research on financial trends,
economic outlook, foreign and domestic financial markets, effects
of government actions, industrial developments, and social trends.
In addition to my weekly report to senior management, I served as
senior editor of "Investment Outlook," prepared by the analysts of
the personal trust division. My analyses of inflation attracted the
attention of the President's Economic Advisory Board and led to my
appointment to Presidential committees noted above. Although on
leave of absence from the Bank of the Pacific when I served on
Presidential committees, I resigned officially to become Chief
Economist, Foundation for American Economic Growth.

ECONOMIC ANALYST, REMINGTON ART AND SCHOOL SUPPLIES, INC., Gary, Indiana,
1960-1965.

This large manufacturer of chalk, crayon, inks, pens, drawing paper,
and other supplies for artists and schools has annual sales of
$150,000,000. It is the parent of three wholly owned subsidiaries.

As economic analyst, I kept the president and treasurer constantly
apprised of the economic environment of the firm and trends of
government, finance, marketing, inflation, labor, raw material
production, and international conditions. In addition, I prepared
special studies on subjects ranging from salary structures to growth
in school populations. When the treasurer of Remington became senior
vice-president of Bank of the Pacific, he invited me to join the
staff of that bank as senior economist.

INSTRUCTOR IN ECONOMICS, METROPOLITAN UNIVERSITY, New York, 1958-1960.

While completing my Doctor of Philosophy degree at Metropolitan, I
taught courses in general economics, monetary policy, and statistics
in the Department of Economics, School of Commerce, Metropolitan
University.

EDUCATION

DOCTOR OF PHILOSOPHY (Ph.D.), ECONOMICS, GRADUATE SCHOOL OF BUSINESS ADMINISTRATION, METROPOLITAN UNIVERSITY, New York, 1957-1960.

Specialized in microeconomic analysis with thesis "Aggregative Thinking in Dynamic Ecological Competition--Three Models."

Granted Straszynski Foundation in Economic Research Fellowship to finance this study, 1958-1959.

MASTER OF ARTS (M.A.), ECONOMICS, GRADUATE SCHOOL OF ARTS AND SCIENCES, METROPOLITAN UNIVERSITY, New York, 1956-1957.

Specialized in social economics with thesis "Impact of Pacific Campaign on Copra Production in South Pacific."

BACHELOR OF ARTS (B.A.), MATHEMATICS, CITY COLLEGE OF NEW YORK (NOW CITY UNIVERSITY), New York, 1952-1956.

MILITARY SERVICE

SERGEANT, INFANTRY, ARMY OF THE UNITED STATES, West Germany, 1948-1952.

PUBLICATIONS

Author, co-author, and editor of over two hundred articles, pamphlets, and studies of scholarly economic research.

AFFILIATIONS

American Economic League
National Association of Microeconomists
Society for the Advancement of Economic Literacy
International Society for the Study of Economics

PERSONAL

Born in Weehawken, New Jersey, March 1, 1930; father an attorney with practice in Jersey City; raised in Weehawken.

Married with three sons, all married; own home in Rye, N.Y.; finances in excellent condition.

Health excellent; 5'9" tall, weigh 160 pounds; no disabilities.

Hobbies travel, hiking, and sailing.

EDITORIAL TRAINING AND EXPERIENCE QUALIFYING
CHARLES BERGERAC
FOR EMPLOYMENT WITH TRADE JOURNAL OR HOUSE ORGAN

6 Virginia Street   Birth: June 1, 1945
Philadelphia, Pa. 07860   Height, Weight: 5'11", 185 lbs.
                                      Health: Excellent
215/665-7642   Marital Status: Married, no children

OBJECTIVE: To serve as managing publisher, editor-in-chief, or
           managing editor of trade journal or house organ.

SPECIALIZATION: Trade journal and house organ editor.

EXPERIENCE

Editor-in-Chief, Textile Plastic Review, 245 Randall Street,
Philadelphia. August, 1972 to Present.

Managing Editor, Beehive, Sterling Insurance Company, 16 State Street,
Philadelphia. July, 1969 to August, 1972.

Reporter, Ocean City Press, Ocean City, Virginia. August, 1968 to
July, 1969.

EDUCATION

Bachelor of Science in Journalism with a minor in Marketing, New York
University. June, 1966.

MILITARY SERVICE

Second Lieutenant, United States Army. July, 1966 to July, 1968.

Information Officer. Responsible for all news services and public
relations at Long Binh Army Base, Vietnam. January, 1968 to July,
1968.

REFERENCES

Mr. R.G. Maxwell, Publisher, Textile Plastic Review, 245 Randall
Street, Philadelphia.

Mr. Louis V. Leventhal, Personnel Director, Sterling Insurance Company,
16 State Street, Philadelphia.

Lt. Col. Harry B. Cain, Information Officer, Fort Dix, N.J.

ENGINEER

TIMOTHY MARTIN

25 Manhattan Parkway
Manhattanville
Alabama 32465

EXPERIENCE AND EDUCATIONAL QUALIFICATIONS IN MECHANICAL ENGINEERING

OBJECTIVE   To obtain challenging position as mechanical design
             engineer in the field of computer building, photocopy
             machine manufacture, or electronic instrument production.

EXPERIENCE   Eight years' experience in mechanical design engineering:

1972-   Supervising Mechanical Design Engineer. PM&K Products,
Present   Montgomery, Alabama, manufacturers of custom-built
             computers, systems groups, and peripheral equipment, with
             annual sales of $90,000,000.

             ● conferred with clients and developed designs of
               computer output devices, sensors, frames, and other
               minicomputer and peripheral equipment.

             ● supervised production of custom-built equipment, with
               follow-up to insure customer satisfaction.

             Company sold out to major computer manufacturer and now
             prepares standardized peripheral equipment. All PM&K
             staff declared redundant and separated.

1970-1972   Mechanical Engineer. Birmingham Electronic Company,
             Birmingham, Alabama, manufacturers of televisions,
             radios, computers, photocopy machines, and cameras, with
             annual sales of $160,000,000. Working primarily in the
             laboratory, I designed and supervised tests for all
             products, gaining great versatility in the areas of
             computer hardware, photographic equipment, and electronic
             instruments.

EDUCATION   Bachelor of Science in Mechanical Engineering (BSME).
             Southern Institute of Technology, Galveston, Texas.
1966-1970   Four-year average of 3.1 on a 4 total.

             ● BSME program notable for incorporation of
               electronic design in the ME program.

             ● Developed and patented magnetic electronic
               device incorporated in a Birmingham
               Electronic computer, as a senior project.

PERSONAL   Born June 1, 1948 in Montgomery; married, 2 children;
             5'11", 180 pounds; excellent health.

REFERENCES   References will be furnished on request.

47

SHIRLEY T. STEDMAN

743 Ninth Street
Armonk, New York 98765
(213) 876 8709

Born July 23, 1947; 5'2", 110 pounds; excellent health, single

OBJECTIVE: To serve as financial analyst with
bank, insurance company, or investment
company.

SUMMARY Ten years of responsible service as financial analyst with
large bank and with insurance company; Master of
Business Administration and Bachelor of Science degrees in
banking and finance; free to relocate anywhere in the
United States or Europe.

EXPERIENCE Investment Analyst, Personal Trust Department, Bank of the
Metropolis, New York City.

1972- Began as research analyst in personal trust research
Present library preparing daily reports on stock market trends;
advanced to research on selected companies, preparing
official reports distributed to bank officers and selected
clients; at present review personal trust client
portfolios, reviewing current investments and making
recommendations for changes in portfolio. Desire change to
gain higher responsibility.

Junior Analyst, Corporate Investment Department, Rivington
Insurance Company, New York City.

1971- Assigned to utilities loan section of this large company's
1972 $10 billion securities portfolio, but oriented in one-year
training program to all phases of Rivington's investments.
Assisted a senior analyst in research on comtemplated
investments, working in research library or in field
inspections and interviews. Left Rivington because I did
not want to specialize in utilities investments.

EDUCATION Master of Business Administration, finance, Graduate School
of Business Administration, New York University.
1969- Specialized in investment analysis, studying
1971 under authorities like Marcus Nadler, Jules Bogen, Douglas
Bellemore, and Siepa Heller.

Bachelor of Science, banking and finance, School of
Commerce, New York University. Studied under such
1965- authorities as Jules Backman, Stanley Studenski, and Martin
1969 Gainsbrugh.

HOBBY Visiting international markets, bourses, and exchanges.

REFERENCES Full references will be furnished on request.

48

FOREMAN, FACTORY

John T. Riley

FOREMAN

25 Glenside Drive
Evertonville
Oregon 09987
(567) 244 9876

47 years old
5'9", 175 pounds
Excellent health
Married, six sons

SUMMARY

INDUSTRIAL FOREMAN with twenty-five years of responsible
leadership experience and with high mechanical aptitude
seeks position in production with manufacturing company.
Evaluations and commendations show outstanding record in
production efficiency, leadership, safety, and labor
relations. Available because last employer, Seattle
Chocolate Company, has gone out of business.

EXPERIENCE   Foreman, Cocoa Department, Seattle Chocolate Company,
Seattle, Washington. Once one of the ten largest
manufacturers of chocolate products in the United States,
this firm discontinued operations in April, 1978.

1963-   Hired on the basis of my ability to keep intricate
1978   machinery functional. I supervised the work of twenty-five
hands operating cocoa presses, pulverizers, and separators,
making fifteen varieties of cocoas and chocolate drinks and
special runs as specified by the laboratory. I had full
authority in hiring and in disciplining employees, training
operators, and establishing hours and shifts. Fullest
harmony with employees and had minimal difficulty with
Grievance Committee since plant was unionized in 1965.

Foreman, Tremount Separators, Inc., Yonkers, New York.
This large East Coast manufacturer is one of America's
principal makers of food processing machinery. At the time
of my employment it had 2,000 employees.

1951-   Hired as a tool and die maker, promoted in two years to the
1963   position of foreman in machine assembly department. Ability
to suggest design modifications and keep production moving
won me the post of assistant night superintendent during
rush periods. Enjoyed full harmony with employees and had
very few cases before Grievance Committee.

1949-   Sergeant, United States Army.
1951

EDUCATION   Graduate of St. Peter's High School, Seattle, 1948; and
Seattle Tool and Die Maker's Institute, 1949.

REFERENCES   Full references and Xerox copies of efficiency ratings will
be furnished on request.

FOREMAN, MECHANIC

GUSTAV HOLTZMAN

<u>FOREMAN</u>

45 Wilbur Drive
Santa Moreno
Florida 24567
(567) 987 5432

<u>AUTO MECHANIC</u>

PERSONAL   Born May 1, 1930; Stuttgart, Germany; U.S. Citizen;
            5'9"; 189 pounds; excellent health; married, children
            adults; finances in excellent condition.

EXPERIENCE Twenty-nine years' experience as foreman mechanic and
            master auto mechanic.

1968-   <u>Foreman Mechanic</u>. Sarasota Motors, Inc. Sarasota,
Present   Florida. Full charge of all repairs and maintenance
            servicing of this $2,000,000 auto agency selling Buicks,
            Volkswagens, and Mercedes-Benz. Supervise the work of
            twenty-five persons including storekeepers and
            and billing clerks.

            Receive all autos brought in by customers; prepare work
            specification records; assign and supervise work;
            perform difficult diagnoses and repairs; check work; and
            submit records for billing.

            Maintain budget; purchase all supplies including parts;
            and hire all mechanics.

            Desire new position because firm is losing lease and
            franchises.

1958-   <u>Foreman Mechanic</u>. Tabanthe Taxi Company, New York,
1968   New York. Supervised crew of twenty-five in maintaining
            large cab fleet. Conducted maintenance checks of all
            cabs; made repairs as needed; supervised all towing,
            bodywork, painting, tune-ups, ignition, transmission and
            preventive maintenance.

            Left this position to relocate family in Florida.

1951-   <u>Mechanic</u>. United States Army Motor Depot, Germany.
1958   Repaired all kinds of American military vehicles.

EDUCATION   Graduate of automotive vocational school in Munich,
            1948. Trained in Mercedes-Benz school, Stuttgart.

REFERENCES Full references will be furnished on request.

CHARLOTTE L. BOSWELL

3245 South Main Street   26 years old
Farmdale, N.Y. 11765   5'5", 123 pounds
(245) 665-0934   Excellent health

---OBJECTIVE---

To serve as a group leader in a chemical, cosmetic, or pharmaceutical
    firm and advance to a production executive post.

---EXPERIENCE---

GROUP   BRANDON-BERN PHARMACEUTICALS, INC., Whiting, N.Y.
LEADER   (1974-Present). Developed and supervised production-line
             group of 40 employees in packaging department. Planned
operation under direction of production vice-president. Recruited and
trained group, which included two registered pharmacists and one
mechanical engineer. Prepared all budgets, production schedules, and
analysis specification checksheets. Promoted for merit from assistant
group leader in container and applicator department.

SUMMER   TRENZIG CHEMICAL COMPANY (a subsidiary of BRANDON-BERN
INTERN   PHARMACEUTICALS, INC.), Morristown, N.J. (Summer 1973).
             Rotated as acting assistant group leader to each of the
product areas of Trenzig Chemical. Spent half time in each cycle as
line worker and half time as staff assistant to group leader. Earned
full-time position with Brandon-Bern after graduation from Seton Hall
University.

---EDUCATION---

BACHELOR   SCHOOL OF BUSINESS AND PUBLIC ADMINISTRATION, SETON HALL
OF SCIENCE   UNIVERSITY (June 1974). Major: Management (Industrial)
             with strong background in chemistry and mathematics.
President of Seton Hall chapter, Society for Advancement of
Management. Earned all living expenses and one-half of tuition as
free-lance typist.

---BACKGROUND---

Born and raised in Passaic, New Jersey, where presence of heavy
    industry inspired industrial career. Both father and mother were
    forepersons in local manufacturing plants. Wrote prize-winning
    essay in college that earned summer intern appointment at Trenzig
    Chemical Company.

---REFERENCES---

References covering both education and experience will be furnished on
    request.

51

MARYLOU HERRMANN

HOME

ECONOMIST

Piedmont Plaza
Garden Heights
Georgia 65432
(345) 346 3478

28 years old; excellent health; 5'5"; 113 pounds; married

Objective

To serve as home economist with food or home products company where my knowledge of home economics, my speaking skill, and my writing ability will be of high value.

Experience

Home Economist, Lyoness Biscuit Company, Mariposa, Georgia, 1975-present. This specialty product baking company distributes mainly in the South. My job is studying consumer preferences, testing feasibility of products catering to these preferences in test kitchen, and reporting results to vice president in charge of research. In addition to reports, I write pamphlets and leaflets for distribution to consumers and make speeches on nutrition before homemaking groups. Desire more responsibility with larger company.

Home Economics Teacher, Mariposa High School, Mariposa, Georgia, 1974-1975. Conducted classes in general home economics covering foods, clothing, and homemaking. Left to work in industry where my true interests lie.

Education

Bachelor of Science, home economics, with minor in journalism, Georgia Agriculture and Technical University, Athens, 1974.

Home Economics Courses	Background Courses
Advanced Nutrition	Writing (five courses)
Home Economics Seminar	Public Speaking (two years)
Test Kitchen Management	Organic Chemistry
Industrial Procedures	Inorganic Chemistry
Professional Cooking	Biochemistry
Food Chemistry	Teaching Methodology
Detergent Chemistry	Survey of Humanities

Background

Born and raised in Georgia; father editor and publisher of weekly newspaper serving farm community; my mother wrote the cooking page; I had a column under my own by-line while I was in college. My husband is a free-lance writer and photographer and is free to relocate with me in any part of the country.

References

Will be forwarded on request.

V I T A

Harrison Jonson
24 Allegheny Avenue
Altoona, Pennsylvania 09876
(123) 456 7890

HOSPITAL ADMINISTRATOR

Professional Objective:

To serve as Chief Administrator of large general hospital.

Experience

WYOMING VALLEY GENERAL HOSPITAL   LAMPORT, PENNSYLVANIA

Acting Chief Administrator. 1976-Present.

Direct all activities of this 200-bed hospital, reporting to
Board of Governors. Engaged as Acting Chief Administrator when
incumbent Chief took year's sabbatical, which was followed by a
serious illness. Incumbent Chief Administrator will return to
hospital in June.

Establish all policies and administrative procedures; oversee the
operation of administrative departments through two assistant
administrators; manage all nonprofessional personnel; supervise
budgeting, special projects, and professional and nonprofessional
training logistics. Represent the hospital in Wyoming Valley
community affairs and participate actively in all community
health projects. Have redesigned admissions systems and billing
activities during past year.

BUCKS COUNTY DOCTORS HOSPITAL   DELAWARE, PENNSYLVANIA

Hospital Administrator. 1973-1976.

Performed all executive functions in this 50-bed hospital,
establishing all goals and directing the activities of all
section supervisors. Revised all billing and admissions
procedures and inculcated a cost-conscious point of view that won
a letter of commendation from Governing Board. Developed a
training program that stressed public relations and greatly
improved image of hospital in community.

HOBSON VETERANS HOSPITAL   INDIANTOWN GAP, PENNSYLVANIA

Assistant Hospital Administrator. 1972-1973.

Designed, implemented, and administered admissions system when
this facility was opened in 1972. Conferring with Chief
Administrator and with architect developed system for patient
reception and processing, allocated corridor and office space,
developed work procedures, selected personnel, and conducted
pilot studies to make system feasible.

Harrison Jonson   -2-

Served as Hospital Training Officer, organizing a training school
and scheduling all classes as specified by Veterans
Administration directives.

Education

PHILADELPHIA CITY UNIVERSITY   PHILADELPHIA, PENNSYLVANIA

Master of Hospital Administration. June, 1967-June, 1970.

Three-year program included one-year administrative residence at
Bucks County Doctors Hospital, Delaware, Pennsylvania.

Academic program included following representative courses:

Basic and Advanced Hospital Management
Hospital and Medical Care Administration
Basic and Advanced Hospital Accounting
Automated Systems in Hospital Administration
Hospital and Community Relations
Hospital Budgeting
Functional Organization of the Modern Hospital
Professional and Nonprofessional Personnel Management

DONEGAL COLLEGE   DONEGAL, PENNSYLVANIA

Bachelor of Science (Biology Major). 1963-1967.

Earned full tuition at college working evenings as orderly and as
clerk in Donegal General Hospital.

Military

UNITED STATES ARMY   MEDICAL SERVICE CORPS

First Lieutenant, Medical Service Corps. June, 1970-June, 1972.

Executive officer in field hospital, Vietnam.

Personal

34 years old; married, 3 children; excellent health; 5'10", 175 pounds

References

References will be forwarded on request. Member of American College
of Hospital Administrators.

INSURANCE CLAIMS ADJUSTER

RALPH REICHERT

Insurance Claims Adjuster

654 Fairmount Terrace, Pittsburgh, Pennsylvania; (345) 678 0987

Personal Details

27 years old
Excellent health
6'2"; 225 pounds

Married, one son
Own home
Finances excellent

JOB OBJECTIVE: Management position in general and casualty
insurance claims investigation and adjustment.

Experience

Claims Adjustment Experience, Claims Adjuster, 1976-Present

Two years of responsible experience in automobile claims with
Hamilton General and Casualty Insurance Company, Pittsburgh.

- Investigate auto accident claims; examine damaged vehicles;
  take pictures, if necessary; interview witnesses and repair
  personnel; complete accident and injury forms

- Report investigations to home office

- Make settlements for claims of $500.00 or less

Managerial Responsibility as Naval Officer, Supply Officer, 1973-1976

Three years of responsibility in Newport and San Diego, supervising
staffs of fifteen to forty-five clerks and enlisted men in
requisitioning, storing, and securing of supplies; inspecting for
quality and security, and administering personnel.

Part-Time and Summer Experience while Attending College, 1969-1973.

Repair and service experience as serviceman with Golden Triangle
Transport Company, Pittsburgh. Earned all tuition for college.

Education

Bachelor of Science, Management, School of Business Administration, Monongahela University, June 1973.

Diversified business training with emphasis on insurance and
finance.

References

Will be furnished on request.

INVESTIGATOR

PAUL GRAGAILLE

(Pronounced GRAY-GUY)

23 MacDougal Road
Phoenix, Arizona   I N V E S T I G A T O R
09876
(123) 456 8907

37 years old; 5'10"; 170 pounds; excellent health; single

PRIVATE INVESTIGATOR with 17 years experience in police, legal,
insurance, and personnel investigation, trained in law enforcement
(AA degree), and skilled in reading public records and financial
statements seeks position with financial institution, law firm,
detective agency, or other investigative organization. Willing to
relocate in any section of United States, no dependents or other
obligations.

PROFESSIONAL INVESTIGATIVE EXPERIENCE:

- **Investigator**, Southwest Security Patrol, Phoenix, 1968 to Present.
  This protective organization will phase out its investigative
  services at end of year and concentrate on security patrols.
  Invited to remain as patrol supervisor, but prefer to remain in
  investigative work.

  During 10 years with Southwest performed following duties:

  Review employment records   Visit banks, schools, public
  of client firms for   agencies in Arizona,
  possible risks in   New Mexico, Nevada, and
  security contracts.   California researching
                                     confidential data for
  Verify data presented by   client firms.
  applicants and current
  information on present   Follow up suspected
  staffs.   defalcations.

- Special Agent, Columbia Banking Company, San Francisco, 1963 to
  1968. During 5 years with this international firm was thoroughly
  trained in personnel background investigation, police and other
  public agency records, review of financial statements,
  interrogation, and fraud detection.

MILITARY INVESTIGATION EXPERIENCE:

Staff Sergeant, Military Police, U.S. Army, Fort Dix and Germany,
1961 to 1963. Plainclothes investigation of civilian backgrounds
of military personnel and sensitive problems in United States and
Europe. Trained in police techniques.

PROFESSIONAL TRAINING IN POLICE INVESTIGATION

Associate in Arts Degree in Law Enforcement, California College of
Government Services, Glendale, June, 1961.

REFERENCES

Full security clearance. References supplied on request.

KEYPUNCH OPERATOR

KEVIN CLEON

Keypunch Operator

34 North Avertine Boulevard, Akron, Ohio 43907, (216) 762-0987

EXPERIENCED KEYPUNCH OPERATOR with both technical school and on-the-job training in computers seeks position that leads to widened computer responsibilities. One year of college. High school diploma. Will relocate.

PERSONAL
22 years old; single, no dependents; 5'7", 165 lbs.; excellent health; born and raised in central Ohio.

EXPERIENCE
Three years part-time and full-time keypunch experience in large corporate data centers.

May, 1976 to Present
MERRICK STANDARDS COMPANY, INC., Akron, Ohio. Heavy 3741/42 experience. Oriented to all alpha and numeric tape and card systems. Trained in maintenance and troubleshooting. Twice commended for mechanical problem solving. Employer knows I am seeking position with wider computer challenge.

May, 1975 to May, 1976
SHELDON REPORTS, INC., Newark, Ohio. IBM 129 experience on five-hour nightshift while attending Dennison University. Experience convinced me that my career lies in computers. Left for full-time computer work.

EDUCATION
One year collegiate training in economics and three months training in computer basics.

1975-1976
DENNISON UNIVERSITY, Granville, Ohio

March-May 1975
SCIOTA TECHNICAL INSTITUTE, Columbus, Ohio

1970-1974
GRANVILLE HIGH SCHOOL, Granville, Ohio. Academic Diploma; electives in typing and all other office machines.

INTERESTS
Mathematics, science, electronics, all sports.

REFERENCES
Mr. Alfred Jones, Vice President, Merrick Standards, Akron, Ohio.

Ms. Mary E. Coughlin, President, Sheldon Reports, Newark, Ohio.

Professor Helen Osborne, Professor of Economics, Dennison University, Granville, Ohio.

57

LABORATORY TECHNICIAN

THORSTEIN ANDERSON--CHEMICAL LABORATORY TECHNICIAN

5236 Elm Street
Otsego, New York 87654
(876) 876 7654

Married, one child; 26 years old; 5'10", 175 pounds; excellent health

JOB OBJECTIVE: position in New York City, Northern
New Jersey, Westchester, or Southern Connecticut
chemical laboratory as laboratory technician.

Experience

Five years of responsible experience as laboratory technician with
Otsego Chocolate Company, 1974-Present. This work is challenging and
very satisfying, but desire to live and work nearer a major city.

• This manufacturer of chocolate and candy products employs 2,500
persons. The chemical laboratory, comprising a staff of twenty-five,
performs research and analytic functions, developing and controlling
quality of products.

• My career with this company has been marked by progressive
advancement in responsibility and remuneration. I started as a
quality control chemist, gathering samples and conducting viscosity
tests in chocolate production. Steadily advanced, I am now in
charge of a team of five responsible for designing formulas for
chocolate runs, distributing packets of special ingredients, and
checking for quality and purity.

Education

Bachelor of Science in chemistry, Southern Connecticut University,
Norwalk, Connecticut. 1974. Honors Program.

Thorough training in chemistry included the following advanced
technical courses:

```
Principles of Chemistry for Honors Students...........9 credits
Organic Chemistry....................................10 credits
Physical Chemistry....................................6 credits
Analytical Chemistry..................................4 credits
Structural Inorganic Chemistry........................3 credits
Chemistry Research for Senior Chemistry Majors........4 credits
```

Professional Articles

"Three Models for Synthetic Vanilla (Non-Vanillin)," Nutritional
Chemistry, Spring, 1980, Volume 15, Number 2, pages 456-500.

"Permyxil and Mahogany Nut Moths," Confectioners Chemistry, May 1981,
Volume 14, Number 5, pages 23-67.

References

References will be furnished on request.

58

LIBRARIAN

Professional Training and Experience of
ALMA STERLING
College Librarian

23 Harrison Boulevard
Fort Benedict Township
Missouri 09876
(345) 462 9078

Born August 1, 1953
5'7", 135 pounds
Single, no dependents
Excellent health

Career Objective: To serve as librarian at a junior or four-year
college or university, participating fully in cultural
activities of that institution

Main Qualifications: Master of Library Science degree (with two
summers of library experience) and Bachelor of Arts degree
in English literature with minor in French literature

Education

Master of Library Science, Randalls University, June 1977, course
included college library internship during summers of 1976 and 1977.

Representative Courses	Description
Foundations of Cataloging	Codes and procedures of Dewey Decimal, Sears and Rue-La Plante, and Library of Congress systems
Organization of the Modern Library	Basic methods for organizing and managing the administrative services of the library
The Library as the Cultural Center of the Community	Review of the services of library to cultural communities with emphasis on university libraries
Summer Internships	Supervised experience in all areas of Randalls University Library-- Basic and Advanced, two summers

Bachelor of Arts, Missouri Technical College, June 1975, in English
literature with minor in French literature. Course included
thorough review of ancient and modern European literature and
American literature, as well as intensive study of English and
French masterpieces.

Experience

Three years of part-time and summer experience as library assistant in
the Fort Benedict Free Public Library keeping records, checking out
books, and maintaining stacks, 1973-1976.

References

Full references will be supplied on request.

MAINTENANCE SUPERINTENDENT

ALFRED FRANCIS
Maintenance Superintendent

2345 MacDougal Street
Chicago, Illinois 45433
(345) 678 9876 (home)
(345) 988 7890 (office)

Born May 1, 1933
5'9", 170 pounds
Married, three sons
Excellent health

MAINTENANCE SUPERINTENDENT, 20 years supervisory experience. Master electrician and stationary engineer licenses; skilled in carpentry, masonry, painting, and landscaping. At present in full charge of maintenance for large Chicago office building but plant is moving to Norfolk, Virginia. Employer knows of desire for new position. Veteran, U.S. Army Engineers.

EXPERIENCE

1968-
present
MAINTENANCE MANAGER, National Discs, Inc., 315 Jay St., Chicago, Illinois. Complete charge of all maintenance of this 38-story facility, including operation of 750-kilowatt diesel generator plant, 1000-horsepower boilers, and 1200-ton refrigerator. Supervise staff of twenty-five. Company wants me to relocate in Norfolk but I prefer to remain in Chicago.

1963-
1968
MAINTENANCE FOREMAN, Ultra-Utility Paper Box Company, 56 Grove Road, Wiltshire, Illinois. Complete charge of maintenance of this 1500-employee plant. Supervised fifteen mechanics and laborers. Kept central power plant and emergency power plant operative; repaired all production machinery; supervised preventive maintenance; repaired and painted interiors and exteriors of buildings; supervised all housekeeping and maintained three acres of landscape. Earned master stationary engineer's license in 1963 while working for Ultra-Utility.

1960-
1963
NIGHTSHIFT MAINTENANCE FOREMAN, Llewellyn Thread and Yarn, Inc., Chicago, Illinois. Supervised two nightshift maintenance crews, a second shift supporting production, a third shift cleaning the idle plant and conducting preventive maintenance. Crews totaled fifty-five men and women during peak periods.

1958-
1960
ELECTRICIAN, Superior Manufacturing Company, Chicago, Illinois. Responsible for all electrical maintenance and repairs. Assisted in rewiring for higher voltage. Earned master electrician's license in 1958 while working for Superior.

EDUCATION

1961   Certificate in Stationary Engineering, State Technical Institute, Chicago, Illinois, attended evenings 1960-1961

1955   High School Equivalency Diploma

1954   Completed apprenticeship as Union Electrician

1952   Graduate of U.S. Army Engineer School, Fort Belvoir, Virginia, qualifying as mason

REFERENCES

Full references will be furnished on request.

MANAGEMENT TRAINEE

<u>GREGORY KAPLOWICZ</u>

24 Palisades Avenue
Clifton, N.J. 09876
(201) 435-8976

Excellent Health
5'9", 168 pounds
22 years old
Single

---OBJECTIVE---

To build a career with a large industrial or financial corporation,
   beginning as a management trainee and earning advancement to a
   top-level management position.

---EDUCATION---

Professionally trained in management practice at two Metropolitan New
   York area colleges.

   GRADUATE MANAGEMENT TRAINING, Graduate School of Business, Seton
      Hall University, South Orange, N.J. Fifteen graduate credits in
      management and management psychology (1980-1981).

   BACHELOR OF SCIENCE in Business Administration, Montclair State
      College, Upper Montclair, N.J. Fully trained in all phases of
      management including accounting, administration, computer science,
      marketing, and office procedures (1976-1980).

---EXPERIENCE---

Professional experience in business practice in full-time, part-time and
   summer positions while attending high school, college, and graduate
   school.

   ASSISTANT MANAGER, Clifton Rubber and Plastics Co., Clifton, N.J.
      Plan and direct the work of 25 clerks in the Customer Order
      Department. Oversee document routing from mailroom, through
      production, to shipping. Prepare operating budget (full time
      1975-present).

   ACCOUNTS RECEIVABLE SUPERVISOR, Passaic Mills, Paterson, N.J.,
      Supervised staff of 6, checked employee accuracy, trained new
      employees, helped install accounting system. Started as part-time
      office boy while in high school, worked summers and part time
      until 1973, started full time 1973 (1972-1975).

---ACHIEVEMENTS---

Developed new system for pinfeeding production forms at Clifton Rubber
   and Plastics that saved $1000 annually; discovered and corrected
   control weakness in billing at Passaic Mills and earned letter of
   commendation from president.

Full references will be furnished on request.

MANAGER

QUALIFICATION SUMMARY OF

MARILYN P. MONTGOMERY

DEPARTMENT OR DIVISION MANAGER

Objective

To join corporation in Columbus, Ohio, area and contribute knowledge, creative insights, and leadership to major department or division requiring imaginative design and control of processed information.

> Twenty-two years' experience as manager of detailed data departments.

> Creator of data-processing and data-storage systems for aircraft manufacturer and for chemical company.

> Manager of staffs of two to three hundred persons, including professional specialists.

> Top-level advisory experience working with first- and second-echelon corporate executives.

> Background in accounting, auditing, contracts, and advertising production.

> Ohio Businesswoman of the Year, 1975.

> Commendations from Governor of Ohio and corporate executives.

> Marital status, single.

A synopsis (qualification) resume is mailed to screen prospects. If response is gained, a fuller resume like one on following page is sent to prospect. See discussion of synopsis resume on pages 153-154.

MARILYN P. MONTGOMERY

Department or Division Manager

Address: 346 Red Cedar Terrace, Columbus, Ohio.   Telephone: 339-6717

Health: Excellent
Height and Weight: 5'6"; 126 pounds
Date of Birth: December 26, 1922
Place of Birth: Carmel, California
Marital Status: Single

MANAGER OF MAJOR DEPARTMENTS, heavy experience data-storage systems, design and management; solid record of creative corporation service; advisory experience with top-echelon corporate management; directed department staffs of two and three hundred, including professional specialists in EDP, research, data retrieval, and advertising production. Own and operate very successful EDP consulting firm, but desire a managerial position in a central Ohio corporation.

OBJECTIVE: To join corporation in Columbus, Ohio, area and contribute knowledge, creative insights, and leadership to major department or division requiring imaginative design and control of processed data.

Experience

EXECUTIVE
EXPERIENCE
Twenty years of managerial experience in data processing, designing creative concepts in three generations of EDP and managing departments of up to three hundred specialists and clerks. This experience included service with the following corporations:

Apexal, Columbus, Ohio. Marketing Director. Directed the work of 200 persons. One-third of this staff were professional specialists in research and advertising production. Reported directly to Mr. Gerald McCaffrey, then President of Apexal. Participated in top-level staff conferences. Invited to become Manager of EDP Operations and Assistant Director of Marketing when Apexal absorbed by Luminale, but preferred to remain in Ohio, where I opened successful EDP consulting firm. (April, 1975-February, 1976)

Griffield Chemical Company, Columbus Plant, Columbus, Ohio. Manager, Records Division. Participated in the design of this division when all corporate records centralized at Ohio Plant; worked with management-consulting firm of Rennes, Campbell, and Dundee in basic systems study and design; recruited operating cadre, and managed this important division--budgeted at one million annually--for seven years; directed work of 300 persons. Value of my service to Griffield attested by fact that Griffield is one of my consulting clients at present. Left Griffield to become Marketing Director of Apexal. (January, 1968-April, 1975)

Griffield Chemical Company, Corporate Headquarters, San Jaime, California. Assistant Manager, Contracts Department. Administered detailed work of 100 employees, reporting to Mr. Ron Blankenship, Manager, an attorney who concentrated on legal aspects of contracts. With Mr. Blankenship, conferred constantly with top-echelon management and with governmental agencies in Washington. Testified three times before Federal government committees. Designed all systems and procedures of department and supervised training of all employees, many of whom were law school graduates. My management skill and data systems creativity earned my promotion to managership of Records Division. (April, 1956--January, 1968)

The Caspian Corporation, San Jaime, California. Internal Auditor, Controller's Department. Serving as first lieutenant to the Director of Auditing Services, helped manage 300 employees. At the time, this large aircraft manufacturer employed 17,000 and was capitalized at $286,827,357. Promoted to this position when Caspian expanded Internal Auditing Section into Operational Auditing Service as result of prizewinning suggestion I submitted to company suggestion system. (January, 1946-April, 1956)

The Caspian Corporation, San Jaime, California. Supervisor, Machine Records Section, Controller's Department. Supervised work of eighty clerks, through day and evening assistant supervisors. Promoted to this position when design I submitted to company suggestion system won installation approval by top corporate management. System described in Business Methods Magazine, June, 1945, which credited me with saving the corporation $15,000 monthly. (January, 1944-January, 1946) Prior to this position served as secretary to Mr. Thomas Sanuk, Executive Vice-President. (June, 1941-January, 1944)

MANAGEMENT   For past two years have operated firm Marilyn P.
CONSULTING   Montgomery, Management Consultant, providing system
              studies and implementation for firms and institutions in
the State of Ohio. This successful firm has served such clients as the Griffield Chemical Company, the George Rogers Clark Hospital, Northern Ohio Wines, Inc., the Litchfield Corporation, and a number of financial institutions. I plan to turn this consulting firm over to my junior partner by the end of the year.

Education

Trained in accounting and management at San Jaime College, awarded Certificate of Proficiency, with honors, June, 1943.

Graduate, Carmel Central High School, Carmel, California, June, 1941.

Honors, Awards, Publications

HONORS AND   Professional honors range from first prize in national
AWARDS FOR   and in California shorthand contests in high school to
PROFESSIONAL election as Ohio Businesswoman of the Year in 1975.
 SERVICES   Officially commended by Governor John Schreiber, Ohio,
             for Chairmanship of the Scioto Valley Ecology Committee.

Commended by Mr. Anthony Griffield, Chairman of the Board, Griffield
Corporation for my assistance to Mr. Ron Blankenship when he appeared
before committee of the United States Senate. Subject of laudatory
article in Executive Woman--"In Ohio, She's Marilyn Our Marilyn,"
August, 1976. Cited in Business Methods Magazine, June, 1945, for
Machine Records System design and fact that I was a Caspian company
supervisor at the age of twenty-one.

PUBLICATIONS Author of many articles in company magazines, of twelve
             company procedure manuals, and of the following articles
             that appeared in national professional journals:

             "Development of Operational Auditing Services,"
             Engineer Auditor, June, 1951. Vol II, No. 15.

             "Centralizing International Records in a Single EDP,"
             Office Procedures Annual, January, 1971. Vol IV, No. 20.

Professional Affiliations

Active membership in the following professional organizations:

             Executive Guild of America
             American Institute of Women Accountants
             Institute of Internal Auditors
             Society for the Advancement of Management
             Ohio Society for Industrial Executives

References

References will be furnished on request.

MEDICAL TECHNOLOGIST

Curriculum Vitae

Loretta R. Campannelli

MEDICAL TECHNOLOGIST

(ASCP Certification)

573 Palmetto Terrace   Excellent health
Sullivant, Virginia   Single
09876   5'4"; 120 pounds
(123) 456 7890   30 years old

objective   To work for large metropolitan hospital with
            convenience to AMA-approved training institution;
            to advance into radioisotope specialization.

experience Eight years general medical technology experience in
            hospitals and private laboratory.

1974-   Shenandoah Hospital and Health Center, Sullivant,
Date   Virginia. Medical Technologist.

            Full charge of all testing in this 125-bed hospital,
            reporting to clinical pathologist. Direct work of two
            technicians whom I have trained. Tests include all
            routine hospital studies of blood, skin, other tissues,
            cultures, and body fluids.

1972-   Richmond Hospital of Physicians and Surgeons, Richmond,
1974   Virginia. Medical Technologist.

            Assisted in radioisotope studies; during 1973
            specialized in blood studies, primarily in blood counts
            and blood cholesterol level studies in this 300-bed
            hospital.

1970-   Richmond Laboratories, Richmond, Virginia. Medical
1972   Technologist.

            Collected samples and conducted routine tests in this
            small private laboratory; work included contact with
            physicians, dental specialists, and patients;
            technician training; and laboratory management.

education   Bachelor of Science (Medical Technology). Central
            University of Virginia. Program included 35 points of
1966-   medical technology; 20 points of general, organic, and
1970   analytic chemistry; anatomy; physiology; histology; and
            bacteriology. AMA-approved program.

certification Registry of Medical Technologists, American Society of
1970   Clinical Pathologists.

references Full references will be furnished on request.

MINORITY MANPOWER SPECIALIST

MARY ELLEN HAMMOND

25 Seymour Fairway
High Ridge, New Jersey 09876
(123) 456 7890

MINORITY MANPOWER SPECIALIST

Objective   To serve as director or assistant director of manpower
              center or manpower project in large corporation.

Experience

Assistant Director, Residential Manpower Center (Job Corps),
Newark, New Jersey, June, 1975 to Present.

- Assisted Director in administering staff of 35 teachers
  and vocational training specialists in operating this
  center for 150 disadvantaged enrollees.

- Directed the processing of 95 enrollees, interviewing,
  testing, guiding, and providing essential services.

- Supervised vocational training of enrollees, scheduling
  classes in English, typing, and stenography.

Employment Counselor, Flying Start Program, New York City,
June, 1972 to June, 1975.

- Interviewed, tested, evaluated, and assigned to training
  and jobs enrollees in this program, which served 120.

- Served as liaison to training groups, social agencies,
  and prospective employers on behalf of enrollees.

Teacher, Commercial Program, North Jersey Vocational School,
Paterson, New Jersey, September, 1970 to June, 1972.

Education

Master of Arts, Virginia Technological Institute, Richmond,
Virginia, June, 1970. Majored in Business Education.

Bachelor of Science, Virginia Technological Institute, June,
1969. Majored in Personnel Management.

Language Skill

Bilingual in Spanish and English

Personal

Born May 1, 1948; single; excellent health; 5'6", 125 pounds.

References

Full references will be furnished on request.

ARISTOTLE SOTER
25 Maplewood Drive
South Orange, N.J.   12345   FINANCIAL ANALYST
(201) 765-4321

Married, No Children   26 years old   5'10", 175 pounds
Permanent U.S. Resident   Fluent English   Excellent Health

OBJECTIVE   To serve as a financial analyst or management trainee
              in a major New York City bank and advance to an
              executive position.

EDUCATION   SCHOOL OF BUSINESS, SETON HALL UNIVERSITY, South Orange,
              N.J., Bachelor of Science, Major: Finance; Minor:
              Accounting. (June, 1980). Average: 3.7/4.0.

1977   Courses include: Advanced Financial Analysis, Advanced
to   Securities Analysis, Advanced Financial Auditing, Cost
1980   and Standards Accounting, Commercial Credit Analysis,
              Executive Banking, International Banking, Applied
              Regression Analysis, National and International Money
              Markets. Earned all expenses through full-time nightshift
              employment at Branch Brook National Bank, Newark.
              Earned all tuition through employment and scholarship.
              Awarded Rathbone Scholarship in third year.

1971   ARISTOTELIAN UNIVERSITY, Salonica, Greece, Bachelor of
to   Laws, Major: Law; Minor: Economics. (October, 1973).
1976   Tuition and expenses financed through Greek National
              Scholarship Foundation Fellowship. Member of Law School
              Student Association and International Relations Club.

EXPERIENCE   BRANCH BROOK NATIONAL BANK, Newark, N.J., Night Manager,
              Data Processing. Supervise staff of 15 computer
1977   specialists. Accept assignments from data processing
to   manager, plan and schedule all work, oversee production,
present   and review performance. Advanced from keypunch operator.

1974   ATHENS COMMERCIAL BANK, Athens, Greece, Trust Officer,
              Legal Advisor. Managed trust accounts, reviewed
              investments, provided legal advice to all departments.

GENERAL   Expect American citizenship October, 1980. Fluent
              English, Greek, and French. Excellent German. Fully
              trained in both American and European accounting.
              Admitted to Athens Bar Association after completion of
              bar examination, January, 1977. Married to natural-born
              American citizen.

              Full references will be furnished on request.

68

JAMES BRUCKNER

908 Parrington Boulevard
Augusta, Maine 09876   Telephone (123) 456 7890

PERSONAL   22 years old; excellent health; 6'1", 180 pounds; single.

OBJECTIVE   To serve a public accounting firm as a junior accountant,
            while I take CPA examinations, and to continue with that
            firm in a public accounting career.

EDUCATION   Bachelor of Science, 1980, Central Maine University
            Major: Accounting (CPA Emphasis)
            Minor: Computer Science

            Representative accounting courses include Current Issues
            in Financial Accounting; Computer-Based Information
            Systems; Advanced Tax Law; and Seminar for Public
            Accountants.

            Representative computer science and business courses
            include Computer Simulation and Modeling; Data-Processing
            Systems; Algorithms, Computers, and Programming; Monetary
            Analysis and Policy; and Foundations of Business.

INTERESTS   Highly active in extracurricular program as undergraduate.

            Professional accounting participation included three
            years in accounting club, treasurer for two years;
            chairman of accounting exhibit at clubs fair, 1979;
            programmer for Statistical Study of Student Programs,
            1979.

            General student activities participation included
            business manager of Central Maine Journal, undergraduate
            newspaper, 1978-1979; class treasurer for all four years;
            co-chairman, senior prom.

BACKGROUND Born in Montreal, Canada, but family moved to Augusta
            when I was seven; United States Citizen; father and
            mother were both schoolteachers in Augusta, until
            retirement last year; I am now engaged to a young woman
            I have known all my life, a senior in elementary education
            at Central Maine.

REFERENCES References will be furnished on request.

Arthur J. Marrone

234 Stryker Avenue   OFFICE
Swansea, New York 09876
(123) 456 7890   ASSISTANT

Objective   To serve as a general assistant in the office of a
                 commercial, industrial, or civic organization, applying
                 my quickness with figures, my typing skill, and my
                 willingness to work hard constantly to increase
                 production and reduction of expense.

Background   Born and raised in Swansea, the youngest of five
                 brothers, all married and employed by Swansea Mills;
                 mother and father both born in Swansea; father a foreman
                 with Swansea Mills where he has worked 30 years;
                 graduate of Swansea High School.

Education   Graduate of Swansea High School, Business Curriculum,
                 June, 1980. Program included following courses:

                      Typing....................3 years
                      Office Machines...........2 years
                      Mathematics...............4 years
                      Bookkeeping...............1 year
                      Business Writing..........1 year
                      Marketing.................1 year
                      Economics.................1 year
                      Salesmanship..............1 semester

                 Program also included general high school courses, with
                 four years of academic English.

Office Skills   Excellent typist (75 words per minute); proficiency in
                 basic office machinery; exceptionally high skill with
                 figures.

Interests   Reading business biographies; mathematical problem
                 solving; chess; Police Athletic League.

Personal   Excellent health; 5'9", 150 pounds; born May 23, 1962;
                 single, no dependents

References   Miss Selma Mansfield, Principal, Swansea High School,
                 45 Hurstboro Drive, Swansea, New York 09876.

                 Mr. Theodore Pomeranki, Head, Business Education,
                 Swansea High School, Swansea, New York 09876.

                 Mr. Eugene Fillmore, Director, Swansea Police Athletic
                 League, and member of Swansea Police Department.

NURSE

Virginia L. Antonelli
1482 Ales Terrace
Glendale, Calif. 90265
213/743-9771

Married, grown children
Born May 2, 1930
Height 5'7", 135 lbs.

OBJECTIVE

To resume career as hospital nurse.

EDUCATION

Refresher Nurse Training	February 6 to March 10, 1977. Pasadena General Hospital, Pasadena, Calif. Eight weeks of intensive refresher training.
Bachelor of Science in Nursing	September, 1959 to June, 1965. Glendale University (evening courses). Full academic training in all phases of general nursing, hospital administration, and supporting sciences, including the following representative courses:

Nutrition   Correlation of nutrition to age, economics, and specific disability.

Junior and Senior Seminars   Relation of nursing to hospital administration, community needs, and general medical science.

Certified as Registered Nurse	September, 1948 to September, 1951. Fully qualified as registered nurse at Los Angeles General Hospital.

EXPERIENCE

Registered Nurse	May, 1973 to April, 1975. Lakeside Nursing Home, Lakeside, Calif. Part-time nurse on duty one evening a week and weekends. June, 1955 to December, 1966. Dr. Albert Simon, 45 Drew Street, Glendale, Calif. Part-time office nurse. June, 1951 to December, 1955. Pasadena General Hospital, Pasadena, Calif. Floor nurse in general and surgical wards, promoted in 1966 to floor head nurse.

HOBBIES

Horticulture, music (play piano and sing).

REFERENCES

Dr. Albert Simon, 45 Drew Street, Glendale, Calif.

Mrs. Martha Torro, R.N., proprietor, Lakeside Nursing Home, Lakeside, Calif.

Dean Hilda Hoffer, School of Nursing, Glendale University, Glendale, Calif.

71

OFFICE MANAGER

ANDRE T. KEMAL

8945 North Fullerton Drive
South Montclair, Delaware 93674
(156) 317-4074

OFFICE MANAGER--COORDINATOR ALL OFFICE SYSTEMS--GOAL ACHIEVER

Office Manager with seventeen years managerial
experience in automobile, insurance, and
public utility companies seeks position in
firm requiring expert knowledge of all office
systems and high production track record.

EXPERIENCE   Heavy management experience directing all office
              work of staffs ranging from 50 to 80 persons in all
              office functions including electronic data processing,
secretarial services, data retrieval, accounting, security, staff
training, switchboard, and project support.

- Director, Central Office Operations. SOLWAY MOTOR,
  LTD., Solway, England. (1976-1980). Designed and
  implemented the Central Office Bureau of this UK
  subsidiary of Champion Motors, Inc. Designed office
  module of EDP system; hired and trained all office
  personnel for staff of 80. Directed all office services.
  Received highest commendations for work. Returned to USA
  when Solway spun off in June, 1978.

- Office Manager. GUIDANCE INSURANCE COMPANY, New York
  City (1968-1976). Managed headquarters office of 50
  data technicians, clerks, and secretaries. Reviewed
  work of 30 office workers in branches. Maintained all
  office accounts. Managed training programs in all areas.

- Branch Manager. WYOMING POWER AND LIGHT, Rawlings Branch,
  (1963-1968). Directed all technical and clerical activities
  of 60 employees. Advanced from position of bookkeeper and
  customer representative in two years.

EDUCATION   Five years continuing education training in EDP and
             office management at NEW YORK UNIVERSITY and in EDP
             applications at NEW YORK ELECTRONIC INSTITUTE. Hold
Associate in Science degree from NEW YORK UNIVERSITY (June, 1961).
Completed five NATIONAL ASSOCIATION OF ACCOUNTANTS seminars.

Full references will be furnished on request.

MARY DESMOND

65 Ocean Avenue
Brooklyn, New York   general office ... typing ...
65432
(212) 456 7890   bookkeeping ... telephone

EFFICIENT, EXPERIENCED OFFICE GENERALIST, ready to take over
full responsibility for operating small office of technical
shop, warehouse, marketer, retailer, or service organization;
cheerful, attractive, and accustomed to one-gal office
operations; available because present employer is moving to South
Jersey.

---

personal

excellent health; age 37; married, adult children; 5'6", 125 lbs.

experience

MANHATTAN BEACH METAL COMPANY   Brooklyn, New York

One-Gal Office Force. Provide all office services in this small
manufacturer of ornamental metal products; assist owner-operator
in planning and general administration; prepare payroll for fifty
employees; keep company books; bill customers; order supplies;
type all documents; receive callers; answer telephone; keep
personnel records; file; and work with public accountant on all
tax returns.

1970-present

GRAVESEND BAY DAIRY COMPANY   Brooklyn, New York

Supervisor, Three-Gal Office Force. Started as one-gal office
force, but given two assistants in 1967; provided owner-operator
with general administrative assistance; helped schedule
activities of 105 employees; supervised and consolidated billing
of route salesmen; prepared payroll; typed documents; operated
key-lite switchboard; and kept books.

1959-1970

KRANDALL'S CLOTHING STORE   Brooklyn, New York

Part-Time One-Gal Office Force. While senior in high school,
worked afternoons and Saturdays keeping books, typing, and
filing--as only office worker--in this ten-employee store.

1958-1959 (afternoons and Saturdays)

Mary Desmond   -2-

education

BROOKLYN COLLEGE   Brooklyn, New York

   Forty-five credits in management, accounting, psychology,
   economics, and general business.

   1960-1962 (evenings)

BROOKLYN COMMERCIAL HIGH SCHOOL   Brooklyn, New York

   Commercial diploma covering bookkeeping, shorthand, typing,
   office practice, commercial arithmetic, and business English.
   Full extracurricular activities including presidencies of
   Merchandise Club, Economics Society, and French Club; treasurer
   of senior class.

   1955-1959

references

Mr. Francis X. Cunningham, Proprietor, Manhattan Beach Metal Company,
56 Coney Island Street, Brooklyn, New York 65432.

Mr. Alphonse Delamoyne (formerly owner-operator Gravesend Bay Dairy),
Proprietor, Coney Island Ice Cream Company, 987 Poseidon Avenue,
Brooklyn, New York 65432.

Mr. Sidney R. Chapman, Manager, Coney Island Branch, New York
Securities Bank and Trust Company, 65 Luna Park Street, Brooklyn, New
York 65420.

hobbies

local history; cycling; exploring Brooklyn; reading; bridge; knitting

TRAINING AND PART-TIME EXPERIENCE OF

SARAH SUE STEELE

SALES CLERK

345 Johnston Road   19 years old
Burlington   5'5", 120 pounds
Vermont 87654   Excellent health
(345) 234 5678   Single

JOB OBJECTIVE: Part-time position as retail sales
clerk, evenings and Saturdays

EXPERIENCE AS SALES CLERK

HIGHWAY 49 DISCOUNT CENTER, Allen, Vermont. Sales Clerk in
Boys' Wear, Books, and Toys. Assisted customers, wrapped
merchandise, and kept shelves in order. Full-time Summer 1979.
Saturdays, September-November 1979; Saturdays and evenings,
December 1979; Saturdays and evenings, January-May 1980.
Resigned to prepare term papers and study for final
examinations.

MACLEOD'S DEPARTMENT STORE, Burlington Vermont; Sales Clerk.
Assisted customers, measured and cut dry goods, vinyls, and
plastic coverings, wrapped merchandise, and served as a checkout
cashier. Summer 1977; Saturdays and Thursday evenings,
September-December 1977 and January-June 1978.

EDUCATION

JUNIOR, VERMONT STATE UNIVERSITY, Burlington, Home Economics
Major. Courses in fabrics, foods, and homemaking tie in with
activities as sales clerk. Honor Roll every term. Free
Saturdays, evenings, and holidays for employment.

GRADUATE, ALLEN HIGH SCHOOL, Academic Diploma. Graduated with
honors. Active in all extracurricular programs.

BACKGROUND

Born and raised in Burlington. Ten years in Girl Scouts.
Sing in church choir. Career objective to serve as home
economist with manufacturing industry.

REFERENCES

Mr. Clarence D. Bullock, Buyer, Highway 49 Discount Center,
Allen, Vermont.

Professor Lawrence C. Parrington, Home Economics Department,
Vermont State University, Burlington, Vermont.

Mr. Thomas K. Campbell, Principal, Allen High School, Allen,
Vermont.

75

PAYROLL CLERK

Alfred Riley

PAYROLL CLERK

15 Orange Street
Yonkers, New York
09876
(914) 456 7890

Born May 30, 1951
Excellent health
5'6", 145 pounds
Single

-----OBJECTIVE--

To provide efficient payroll preparation services to
large organization and to develop into wage and
salary administrator or related managerial position.

----------------------------EXPERIENCE----------------------------

Payroll Astor Novelty Goods Company, New York City; distributors of
Clerk   gift and premium novelties. 1974-Present.

Prepare payroll for 70 employees according to schedule which I
helped develop with the General Manager.

Assist in personnel and bookkeeping as needed.

Desire larger growth opportunity.

Sales   Ni-Phi Wholesale Toy Company, New York City; distributors of
Clerk   children's toys and games. 1969-1974.

Began as stock clerk but promoted to sales clerk. Received
buyers, discussed needs, demonstrated merchandise, and filled
orders. Typed payroll and tax reports.

----------------------------EDUCATION----------------------------

Hamstrom Business Institute, New York City, evenings, 1972-1974.

Personnel Administration   Wage and Salary Administration
Machine Accounting   Business Administration

Minuet High School of Commerce, 1965-1969, Commercial Diploma.

----------------------------SKILLS----------------------------

Full knowledge of payroll taxes and deductions
Ability to operate standard bookkeeping machines
Expert typist

----------------------------REFERENCES----------------------------

References will be furnished on request.

76

PROFESSIONAL QUALIFICATIONS OF

JOHN PIERCE

FOR PERSONNEL ADMINISTRATION OR INDUSTRIAL RELATIONS

230 Matawah Boulevard   Born May 1, 1945
Raritan Township   6'2", 190 pounds
New Jersey 09876   Excellent health
(201) 345 6789   Single

PERSONNEL AND INDUSTRIAL RELATIONS ADMINISTRATOR, trained in
personnel, labor relations, and law, with experience in both
personnel management and industrial relations, seeks personnel
administrative position with large industrial or service
organization. Willing to locate anywhere in the United States.

EXPERIENCE

Twelve years of progressive experience in personnel and industrial
relations--1968-Present.

1974-   Manager of Industrial Relations, Masterson-Brent Electric
Present   Company, Elizabeth, New Jersey. Complete charge of all labor
            relations between this manufacturer of electric motors and its
            500 union workers. Report directly to Vice President,
            Personnel. Collaborate with Personnel Department in
            establishing labor policy, negotiate labor contracts,
            participate on grievance committees, maintain records, insure
            fair hiring practices, and check all labor transactions to
            insure conformity with law. Supervise staff of eight.

1970-   Assistant Manager of Personnel, Ambo Coffee Company, Brooklyn,
1974   New York. This Brazilian-based firm employs 2000 office and
            warehouse workers in its Brooklyn facility. I supervised a
            staff of six interviewers and testers for hiring both office
            and warehouse personnel. In addition, my staff maintained
            all records for warehouse personnel and devised policy for
            training, rating, and disciplining skilled and unskilled
            workers.

1968-   Placement Office Intern, St. Regis College, Short Hills,
1970   New Jersey. While completing my Bachelor of Laws at St.
            Regis, I assisted the Director of Placement in scheduling the
            visits of 150 companies in on-campus recruiting.

EDUCATION

Bachelor of Laws, St. Regis College, Short Hills, New Jersey, June 1970.
   Degree conferred with honors. Admitted to New Jersey Bar 1971.

Bachelor of Science, Management, St. Regis University, June 1966.

MILITARY

Military Occupation Assignment Clerk (Spec. 2), Saigon, 1966-1968.

REFERENCES

Full references will be forwarded on request.

John L. Bruiac

REGISTERED PHARMACIST

1450 Adirondack Avenue, Syracuse, New York, 12345; (123) 456 7890

Objective	To manage prescription department of large pharmacy in department store or chain retail organization.
Experience	Center Street Pharmacy, 230 Center Street, Syracuse, New York. Pharmacist-in-Charge. 1974-Present. ● Coordinate pharmacy operations with overall store operations. ● Supervise work of three pharmacists and five clerks. Fill prescriptions. ● Purchase all stock and maintain all drug inventories. Interview salesmen. ● Supervise all point-of-purchase merchandising. Prepare advertising. Blaine's Department Store Pharmacy, 50 Genessee Street, Syracuse, New York. Advanced from Pharmacist to Manager of Drug Department. 1970-1974.
Education	Bachelor of Pharmacy, School of Pharmacy, Penyan University, Penyan, New York. 1969. Internship, Syr-Ute Pharmacy, State Street, Utica, New York, 1969-1970.
Professional License	Licensed to practice pharmacy in State of New York (examination passed, 1971).
Financial Condition	Personal finances in excellent condition; in position to invest substantially in pharmacy or pharmacy department. Can furnish excellent bank references.
Personal	Married, 2 children, 32 years old, excellent health, 5'7", 150 pounds. Own home free and clear.
References	Full references will be furnished.

78

V I T A

ARTHUR M. BAKELESS, M.D.

    4 Kenmore Hollow   Industrial Medical Director
Riverside, Maine 09876
    (123) 456 7890

40 years old; excellent health; 5'10", 165 pounds; married, 2 children

        OBJECTIVE: To serve as Medical Director of large
                   industrial firm; willing to locate in
                   any part of continental United States.

EXPERIENCE

Assistant   Pennecott Paper Products, Inc., Pennecott, Maine, 1972 to
Medical   date. Pennecott and wholly owned subsidiary North Maine
Director   Lumber Company employ 20,000 workers in paper mills,
            lumber mills, and forests of Maine. Desire new post
because Pennecott is selling North Maine Lumber, making post of
Assistant Medical Director unnecessary. As Assistant Medical Director,
have responsibility for three other physicians and twenty nurses,
clerks, and technicians at the following facilities:

    Lumber Camp Hospital and Clinic. With help of industrial
    physician, conduct physical examinations and treat all injuries
    sustained in lumber camp and forests.

    Industrial Hospital. With help of industrial physician, treat and
    rehabilitate illness and injuries transferred from Lumber Camp
    Hospital and Paper Mill Dispensary.

Industrial Conshonken Chemical Company, Newark, New Jersey, 1965-
Physician   1972. Conshonken employs 3,500 workers in the Ironbound
           Section of Newark. The medical staff consisted of five
other physicians and twenty nurses, clerks, and technicians. During my
service with Conshonken, conducted physical examinations, evaluated
employee health problems, treated injuries, administered Workmen's
Compensation, and prepared internal hygienic programs and environmental
improvement concepts. Served as Acting Assistant Medical Director in
1972.

EDUCATION

Doctor of Medicine, New York University School of Medicine, New York
    City, 1964. Internship at St. James Hospital, Newark, New Jersey,
    1964-1965. Licensed to practice in New Jersey (1965); New York
    (1966); and Maine (1971).

Bachelor of Arts, Seton Hall University, South Orange, New Jersey,
    1956-1960. Earned my full tuition working evenings in plastics
    manufacturing plant in the Ironbound Section of Newark.

REFERENCES

References will be furnished on request.

PRODUCT MANAGER

EXPERIENCE AND TRAINING QUALIFICATIONS OF
JOHN C. WHITTLE
FOR POSITION AS RECREATION PRODUCTS MANAGER

245 North Alpine Drive; Highlands, New Jersey 24567; (201) 345 6789

OBJECTIVE: Position of product manager in the sporting goods or recreational field where my marketing training and experience, my knowledge of the recreational field, and my creative sales-promotional talents will find full challenge; former member of US Olympic Team.

EXPERIENCE PRODUCT MANAGER, GYMCO COMPANY, Newton, New Jersey

1973-
Present
This manufacturer of gymnastic equipment has annual sales of $120,000,000. It distributes directly and through wholesalers, jobbers, and retailers such products as basketball nets, roman rings, parallel bars, mats, and exercising devices.

As product manager, I collaborate with sales manager in developing marketing and sales promotion plans for various gymnastic devices. I coordinate and budget efforts of design, promotion, and sales personnel. I research consumer preferences and arrange demonstrations at fairs, special events, department stores and gymnasiums. I increase sales by 500% in most of the products I upgrade.

Desire new position because I want more independence in designing and developing products.

1965-
1973
PRODUCT MANAGER, SUN AND SNOW ATHLETIC EQUIPMENT, Astoria, New York (Subsidiary of German-based TURNVEREIN INDUSTRIES, Hamburg)

This large German manufacturer of sporting equipment launched an American line in 1966. Working with the manager of the Astoria plant, I tested for market acceptability the full product line and selected the gymnastic equipment, skis, and ski boots that I found had ready sales in America. Working in both Hamburg and Astoria, I helped adapt these products to the American market. I collaborated in all promotion and selling of these products. I left because distribution, once successfully launched, became routinized.

EDUCATION Bachelor of Science, Recreational and Health Education, with minor Distributive Education, Teacher's College,
1965 Metropolitan University, New York City. Captain of gymnastic team; member of baseball and soccer teams.

PERSONAL Born June 1, 1943; 5'10", 165 pounds; married; excellent health; member of U.S. Olympic Team, parallel bars, 1963.

REFERENCES References will be furnished on request.

80

PUBLIC RELATIONS DIRECTOR

ALEXANDER C. PHELAN
54 Fenimore Way
Oakland, California 09876
(123) 456 7890

PUBLIC RELATIONS DIRECTOR with top-level corporate experience;
heavy staff advisory, policy-building, and administrative
responsibility; excellent writer and speaker; and strong
editorial background, available to direct public relations
department of large West Coast corporation.

---PRESENT POSITION--

Director of Public Information, Cruise-Craft, Inc., Oakland, 1974
to Present. This major builder of watercraft from rowboats to
yachts employs 8000 persons and has sales of one and one-half
billion dollars annually. Corporate offices are moving to New York
City in April, but I prefer to remain on West Coast.

Administrative Responsibilities

● Direct all activities of Public Information Department
  consisting of fifty editors, staff writers, and research
  specialists.

● Serve as Editor-in-Chief of promotion magazine Cruise-Craft
  World and house organ Cruise-Craft House Boat, directing the
  work of special editorial staff and production workers.

Company Representation

● Represent company before national and state government
  bodies, including state legislatures, to present company
  point of view on pending regulations.

● Represent company at conventions and other meetings of
  businessmen and professional groups.

● Represent company before civic groups in San Francisco Bay
  area and in lake and maritime regions.

Staff Advisory Duties

● Advise President of Cruise-Craft constantly of public
  relations implications of all current and proposed projects.

● Confer with Executive Committee constantly in reviewing
  current programs, in developing new courses of action, and
  in setting policy.

● Assist major executives in development of public statements
  and articles.

● Confer with department heads on ways to implement public
  relations policy.

81

---PREVIOUS POSITIONS---

Public Relations Manager, California Utilities Advisory Group,
Sacramento, 1970-1974. This consulting and service firm provides
counsel, labor negotiating services, and legislative representation
to 1000 firms and trade associations in the Far West. It has a
staff of 300.

Public Relations and Editorial Responsibility

- Directed staff of eight in publication of journal Far West
Utilities issued monthly to clients and their management
staffs.

- Prepared, with aid of staff, all releases, articles,
pamphlets, and other literature for clients.

- Maintained contact with West Coast media, issuing information
and arranging news and feature article coverage of client
activities.

Advisory Responsibility

- Served on second-echelon staff as advisor to group.

- Conferred with clients on their public relations problems.

City Editor, Sacramento Mountain Dispatch, 1965 to 1970.

Reporter and Rewriter, San Francisco Observer, 1959 to 1965.

---EDUCATION---

Bachelor of Science, West Coast University, Oakland, California,
June, 1959. Majored in Political Science, earned all tuition
working evenings as reporter and rewrite man for Oakland News
Chronicle.

---PERSONAL--

Born May 15, 1937; married, three adult daughters; excellent
health, 5'10", 170 pounds; finances in excellent condition.

---REFERENCES--

Outstanding references will be furnished on request.

PURCHASING MANAGER

Charles P. Huang
44 Saskatchewan Boulevard
Paris Lake, Georgia 98760
(123) 456 7890

P U R C H A S I N G

M A N A G E R

PERSONAL
Date of Birth: August 1, 1944
Place of Birth: Atlanta, Georgia
Marital Status: Married, one son
Height and Weight: 5'11", 175 pounds
Health: Excellent

OBJECTIVE

To direct all purchasing in chemical, electronic, or other technically oriented manufacturing company.

EXPERIENCE

Twelve years' experience as purchasing manager for technically oriented manufacturers, both positions requiring scientific academic background.

- Martigny Pharmaceutical Company, Atlanta, Georgia, Director of Purchasing, 1971 to Present. Large Southern firm, employing 10,000, being consolidated with Sion Chemical Company, Atlanta, at end of year. Invited to remain as member of purchasing team, but prefer a managerial post. Direct activities of Purchasing Department of 15 employees. Purchase $75 million in chemicals, production equipment, supplies, and furniture annually, receiving salesmen or calling upon sources. Confer with laboratory and production staffs and technical staffs of vendors. Track all sources of material and visit European, South American, and African markets.

- Reliability Electronics Company, Parker, South Carolina, advanced from Purchasing Agent to Purchasing Manager, 1968 to 1971. Left this manufacturer of electronic instruments, 3,000 employees, to become Director of Purchasing at Martigny. Rapid advancement came primarily from ability to translate needs of scientific staff into high-quality, low-cost purchases.

EDUCATION

Thorough training in chemistry, electronics, and marketing.

- Master of Business Administration (Marketing), Johnston University, Atlanta, Georgia, June 1968.

- Bachelor of Science (Major, Chemistry; Minor, Electronics) Johnston University, Atlanta, Georgia, June 1967.

————————PUBLICATIONS————————

Five articles contributed to professional journals on technical purchasing and on overseas raw material sources.

- "The Purchasing Agent Assists in Instrument Development," Journal of Therapeutic Techniques, Summer, 1980; Vol. 45, No. 15; pp. 17-64.

- "Trends in Abyssinian Civet Production," Overseas Markets, December, 1979; Anniversary Issue, Vol. 50; pp. 63-89.

- "Substitutes for Coal Tar Available on Swiss Markets," The Journal of Chemical Synthesis, Spring, 1975; Vol. 10, No. 14; pp. 14-27.

- "The Purchasing Director on the Product Team," Industry Notes, May, 1974; Vol. 3, No. 7; pp. 5-19.

- "Purchasing as a Mirror Image of Selling," Modern Purchasing, September, 1973; Vol. 15; No. 5; pp. 14-21.

————————PROFESSIONAL AFFILIATION————————

Past president of Southern United States Purchasing League (1976); Member of American Purchasing Agents' Association (1968-Present); Member of Swiss-American Pharmaceutical Alliance (1974-Present).

REFERENCES

- Mr. Albert Kohler, President, Martigny Pharmaceutical Company, 123 Peach Tree Street, Atlanta, Georgia 09876

- Mr. Howard Vallazzo, President, Reliability Electronics Company, 450 Grove Avenue, Parker, South Carolina 08796

- Dr. Chauncey Desmond, Chancellor, Johnston University, East Elm Road, Atlanta, Georgia 09876

ARTHUR D. SOFFAIR
200 Silverton Circle
Chicago, Illinois 60604
(312) 456-9876

Married--One child
32 years old
Excellent Health
5'6", 140 lbs.

---OBJECTIVE---

To serve as a Quality Control Assurance Manager with a manufacturer
    or industrial engineering company and advance to an executive
    position in production.

---EXPERIENCE---

Over six years' experience in quality control supervision with two
    major American manufacturers.

- Quality Control Supervisor. PEDERSEN-BRYANT, INC., Geary,
  Illinois Plant (1976-Present). Supervised staff of 35
  inspectors in electronic trip-up department; managed routine
  testing of five standard components and special testing of
  tailored assemblies; served as reliability member of
  production team; and regulated the quality control adjustments
  of six foremen. A cost and standards review credited me with
  a 67% improvement in production efficiency.

- Quality Assurance Engineer. DREN-DIE TOOLING CO., Delawanna,
  New Jersey (1974-1976). Controlled all reliability through all
  production cycles from purchasing to client delivery; reviewed
  client and government specifications; developed and supervised
  appropriate tests; recruited and trained all inspectors and
  testers; managed all documentation.

---EDUCATION---

Thorough training in management and mechanical engineering.

- Master of Business Administration. GRADUATE SCHOOL OF
  BUSINESS ADMINISTRATION, NEW YORK UNIVERSITY (June, 1974).
  Major: Industrial Management.

- Bachelor of Science in Mechanical Engineering. OHIO STATE
  UNIVERSITY (June, 1972).

---ASSOCIATIONS---

Member of the American Association of Quality Assurance Engineers and
    the American Society of Mechanical Engineers.

---REFERENCES---

References will be furnished on request.

REAL ESTATE SALESPERSON

J. OLIVER BENNETT
Real Estate Salesman

89 Marlene Boulevard
Union, New Jersey 09876
(201) 409 8769

27 years old
Married; son 5
6'1", 185 pounds
Excellent health

PROFESSIONALLY QUALIFIED REAL ESTATE SALESMAN with Broker's
License, university degree in real estate, and ten years of
successful full-time and part-time sales experience seeks sales
position with dynamic New Jersey real estate firm.

EXPERIENCE

1975-
Present

Real Estate Salesman, Mirabelli Associates, Scotch
Plains, New Jersey. This $1,000,000 realty firm develops
housing tracts, manages over 1,000 properties, and sells
both residential and industrial real estate.

Sold both industrial and residential properties in North
and Central New Jersey; called upon industrial sellers
and buyers, assisted appraisers, arranged both finance
and insurance, and assisted at major closings; helped
arrange housing tract developments, cooperating with
builders and financial institutions from time of title
search to closing; appraised and sold private homes in
Wyoming Avenue, Ridgewood Avenue, Upper Mountain Avenue,
Hawk's Nest, and Englewood Cliffs areas. Desire new
position because firm is being reorganized into three
independent companies.

1972-
1975

Real Estate Salesman, Arthur C. Murray, Realtors,
Rutherford, New Jersey. This small realty firm consists
of a proprietor, three salesmen, and an office assistant,
and specializes in homes in the Rutherford, Nutley, and
Bloomfield areas.

Sold and appraised residential real estate and arranged
financing through banks and savings and loan associations.
Learned principles of surveying from one of the salesmen
who was a retired civil engineer. Outstanding sales
success, but desired wider scope experience in properties
sold and services provided.

Part-time
1970-
1972

New Home Salesman, L.G. Bauer, Inc., Builders, Union,
New Jersey. This $750,000 company develops residential
tracts in North Jersey. I worked evenings and weekends
while in college showing the model homes of these
developments.

EDUCATION
1968-
1972

Bachelor of Science, Real Estate, St. Lioba College,
Livingston, New Jersey. Thoroughly trained in all phases
of real estate.

BROKER'S
LICENSE

Granted Broker's License in 1973.

REFERENCES

References will be furnished on request.

Mary
  Ann
    NOVAK------------------------------------- R E C E P T I O N I S T

        300 Parapet Drive
        Cyres
        Tennessee 98765
        (321) 445 9876

Personal: excellent health, 5'6", 120 pounds
          single
          eighteen years old

Objective to serve as receptionist, preferably in executive suite
          of large corporation.

Education
Graduate, Cyres High School, June, 1980, commercial course.

    Grade of "A" in all business courses

        Introduction to Business   Salesmanship
        Office Practice   Business Mathematics
        Typewriting, three years   Business English
        Shorthand, two years   Secretarial Science
        Bookkeeping   Office Machines

    Overall grade of "B+." Full extracurricular participation.

Experience
Demonstrator, Glissade Refrigerator Company, Saturdays, September-June
    1979-1980, and Summer 1979. Appeared at department stores in
    Tennessee, Louisiana, and Texas and at county and state fairs.
    Appeared in two television demonstrations.

Sales Clerk, Cyres Department Store, Cyres, Tennessee, Thursday
    evenings and Saturdays, September-June 1978-1979.

Receptionist, Chronique Watch Company, Cyres, Tennessee, Summer 1978.
    Served as relief receptionist on three different floors. Filled in
    as receptionist to president when his receptionist was on vacation.
    Served as a model in two Chronique advertisements in Sunday
    supplements of newspapers, including the New York Times.

References

Mr. Merriwether C. Delaney, President, Chronique Watch Company,
    28 Insurance Plaza, Cyres, Tennessee.

Mr. Thomas Harding, Manager, Special Exhibits, Glissade Refrigerator
    Company, Dallas, Texas.

Mr. Leland Cox, Principal, Cyres High School, Hauxhurst Avenue,
    Cyres, Tennessee.

RECREATION DIRECTOR

<u>EXPERIENCE, TRAINING, AND SENSITIVITY QUALIFICATIONS</u>

J O H N T. B R A N N A R

PLAYGROUND AND RECREATION DIRECTOR

245 Elmwood Avenue, Detroit, Michigan 23456; (234) 567 8902

Personal Details

<u>Born</u>:	March 19, 1947	<u>Place of Birth</u>:	Detroit
<u>Health</u>:	Excellent	<u>Marital Status</u>:	Single
<u>Height</u>:	6'3"	<u>Dependents</u>:	None
<u>Weight</u>:	210 pounds	<u>Profession</u>:	Teacher

<u>OBJECTIVE</u>: To serve as a summer and Saturday director of a playground in the Detroit area.

<u>SUMMARY</u>: Eighth Grade Teacher in Wilson Avenue School, Detroit, Michigan; BA and MA degree, with strong experience in recreation and athletics and 24 points in physical education; capable of organizing program tailored to neighborhood needs; full knowledge of equipment, games, health development, dances and songs.

Experience

<u>PRESENT FULL-TIME POSITION</u>

Licensed, tenured teacher in Wilson Avenue School, specialization English, serve as dramatic coach; have staged three school shows and one faculty show. 1973-Present.

<u>MILITARY RECREATIONAL EXPERIENCE</u>

Corporal, Recreation and Rehabilitation Center, United States Army, Honolulu, Hawaii, 1970-1973.

<u>PART-TIME AND SUMMER RECREATIONAL EXPERIENCE</u>

<u>Athletic Director</u>, Moose Antler Lake Camp, Moose Antler, New York, Summers 1973, 1974, 1976. (Attended summer school 1975).

<u>Camp Counselor</u>, Camp Lake Clear, Lake Clear, New York. Summers 1967, 1968.

<u>Recreational Assistant</u>, Sylvester Park Playground, Detroit, Summers and Saturdays 1965, 1966.

Education

Master of Arts, Guidance and Counseling, Fort Dearborn University, Fort Dearborn, Illinois, 1970. Took three electives in Physical Education.

Bachelor of Arts, English, Fort Dearborn University, Fort Dearborn, Illinois, 1969. (Matriculated originally as Physical Education Major.) Played Varsity Football 1966, 1967, 1968.

References

Will be furnished on request.

HELENA T. SIMMS

45 Spruce Drive
East Illini, Illinois
24567
(234) 567 8910

PORTFOLIO ANALYST

REGISTERED REPRESENTATIVE

Age: 25
Health: Excellent
Height and Weight: 5'6", 130 pounds
Marital Status: Single, no dependents

IMMEDIATE OBJECTIVE: To provide full-scale client services to customers of stockbroker, investment house, or trust division of bank through market-trend insights, portfolio analysis, written reports, and client contact.

CAREER OBJECTIVE: To assume increasing executive responsibility in investment administration.

EXPERIENCE

Registered Representative, Powers and Stanley, Incorporated, Members of New York Stock Exchange, New York City and Chicago offices, December, 1976 to present. Heavy experience in portfolio analysis and report writing, dealing particularly with computerized valuations and sales programs. Desire change because recent consolidation limits advancement opportunity.

Trainee, Haberstroh, Sargeant, Inc., Members of New York Stock Exchange, 109 Broadway, New York City, December, 1975 to December, 1976. During year's employment with this stockbroker, took six months' correspondence course to qualify as Registered Representative. Passed qualifying test given by New York Stock Exchange. Took in-house courses in investment analysis, market trends, public speaking, and customer relations.

Secretary, National Federation Bank, Corporate Trust Division, Nine Broad Street, New York City, June, 1971 to May, 1975. Performed general secretarial duties for Senior Vice-President; assisted in preparation of market-analysis reports.

EDUCATION

Bachelor of Science degree in Banking and Finance, New York University, College of Business and Public Administration, June, 1975. Attended evenings while serving as secretary at National Federation Bank. Graduated magna cum laude, elected to Beta Gamma Sigma in junior year.

Graduate of Marshall Field High School, Chicago, June, 1971.

REFERENCES

References will be furnished on request.

MAIN QUALIFICATIONS OF CHARLES A. TRENT--<u>RESTAURANT MANAGER</u>

> 335 Stratford Parkway
> Murray Hill
> New Jersey 07004
> (201) 234 5678

At present manager of well-known New Jersey restaurant
grossing $300,000 a year, being purchased by chain.

Twenty-seven years of top-flight restaurant experience,
including ownership of Gaslight Restaurant, sold at
a 200% gain in profit.

Once chef of New York-Shropshire Hotel.

Married, finances in excellent condition.

Ready to relocate in any part of the country.

Excellent appearance. Can speak French, German, and
Italian.

Natural-born United States citizen.

FULL RESUME WILL BE FORWARDED ON REQUEST.

A synopsis (qualification) resume is mailed to screen
prospects. If response is gained, a fuller resume like one on
following page is sent to prospect. See discussion of
synopsis resume on pages 153-154.

CHARLES A. TRENT

335 Stratford Parkway   <u>RESTAURANT</u>
Murray Hill
New Jersey 07004   <u>MANAGER</u>
(201) 234 5678

Objective: To manage large, quality food restaurant or large
             restaurant in hotel.

SUMMARY OF MAIN QUALIFICATIONS

RESTAURATEUR, thoroughly trained in all phases of top-flight
restaurant operation, with thirty years' experience as manager, chef,
wine steward, and restaurant owner. Excellent appearance, suave, with
working knowledge of French, German, Spanish, and Italian.

EXPERIENCE

<u>Manager</u>, <u>Duke of Wellington Tavern</u>, Wellington, New Jersey,
1972-Present. Annual Sales, $300,000. Personnel, 85.

Engaged to reestablish the reputation of this famous restaurant,
dating back to 1825. Worked with architect on the remodeling of the
old building, prepared layout for kitchen, dining room, and dining
porches. Hired chef and assistant chef and retrained staff.
Redesigned menu, replacing a wide, uneconomical variety of
undistinguished offerings with a restricted selection of high-quality
foods. Expanded the beverage department and installed an excellent
wine cellar.

Have complete charge of all operations including purchases, collection
of cash, menus, and personnel since opening. Desire change because
restaurant is being purchased by a national chain with centralized
management and standardized procedures.

<u>Manager</u>, <u>Old Vienna Restaurant</u>, Floral Park, Long Island, 1962-1972.
Annual sales, $250,000. Personnel, 65.

Hired as chef in 1962, but promoted to assistant manager and wine
steward the next year and to manager in 1964. At the request of the
owner, I continued to supervise all food preparation closely and
helped maintain a reputation for quality cuisine that I had
established as chef. Despite time spent in supervising the kitchen
and food service, I had full charge of all purchases, personnel, and
cash intake. Left to work at Duke of Wellington because I wanted more
independence.

<u>Proprietor</u>, <u>Gaslight Restaurant</u>, Port Jervis, New York, 1955-1962.
Annual Sales, $100,000. Personnel, 25.

91

Charles A. Trent   -2-

Opened this restaurant on very small scale with my wife and two
cousins. Restaurant quickly earned outstanding reputation for
excellent cuisine.

I served as both chef and manager, even after the restaurant
succeeded. My wife opened a small baked goods outlet in 1960 and sold
goods that she and I baked. We sold this restaurant in 1962 at a 200%
gain in profit.

Chef, New York-Shropshire Hotel, New York, New York, 1951-1955.

Hired as assistant chef, but promoted to chef in 1953. As chef,
supervised staff of 35, made all purchases, and supervised preparation
of 2,000 meals daily. Designed all menus. This hotel restaurant was
awarded first prize by Tourist Magazine every year that I was chef.
Left because I wanted to own my own restaurant.

MILITARY

Cook with rank of technical sergeant, Army of the United States,
1946-1951. Completed four-month course in Cook and Bakers School,
Governor's Island, New York. Retained as instructor for one year and
then served in Europe.

EDUCATION

Attended school in United States, France, Spain, and Italy, traveling
with father who was an overseas representative of American firms.

PERSONAL

Born January 1, 1925; married, two married daughters; excellent
health; 6'1", 190 pounds; finances in excellent condition.

REFERENCES

References will be furnished on request.

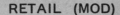

RETAIL (MOD)

```
D
 o
  l   N I C H O L A U S
   p
    h
```

MAD MOD (thoroughly mod) RETAIL MANAGER

PAD, etc...   BIRTH TO GIRTH, etc...

45 Carl Schurz Avenue   Health: To Spare
Milwaukee, Wisconsin   Post-Gap Birth: May 1, 1960
98765   Length and Gravity: 5'10", 150 pounds
(345) 276 9876   Marital Status: Heavens Forbid!
                                    Personality: Really With It

THOROUGHLY HIP RETAIL-MINDED GUY, iconoclastic tendencies, but
thoroughly trained in retail operations and business methods
(before liberation) and creatively oriented to psychedelic
tastes, stock, shock, and decor, ready to establish dialogue with
and please the clockwork tangerine whims of mod clothing, art,
music, and antidisestablishmentarian impedimenta, etc.,
Carnaby-type clientele.

Balance Sheet of Virtues and Vices

Virtues	Vices
Two years' experience as sales clerk and manager of psychedelic clothing and art-music shops.	Hang-up for profitability; somehow stores I manage make profits that embarrass owners all the way to the bank.
Pendelton's, Chicago. 1978-1980 Buss-Mill Shop, London. 1979 Haverton's, New York. 1978 Thorough knowledge of mod art, music, literature, and tastes.	Hang-up for behind-the-scenes efficiencies. Study clientele tastes, contrive insidious decors that induce buying, drive shrewd bargains with vendors' salespeople.
Ability to design epicene garments and thoroughly camp bric-a-brac.	Precocious kook with BS in retailing at age 19 from Northern Plains University. (1977)
Love to spend time with people.	Love to have people spend money in my stores.

If you would like to meet me despite these eradicable
vices and want a few references, just holler, man!

ROBERT G. STERN
Sales Representative

College Address	Permanent Address
234-C Highland Dormitory Franklin Technical College Brownsville, Texas 09876 (345) 456 7890 Ext. 234-C	2345 Kennedy Boulevard Ainsworthy Township Texas 90678 (345) 543 9078

MARKETING MAJOR, with Bachelor of Science expected June 1978, desires position as sales representative for food corporation distributing through supermarkets, department stores, and retail stores in shopping centers. Six years of summer and parttime experience in supermarkets and department stores. Excellent appearance and first-rate sales personality. Interested in marketing career with the right company.

PERSONAL
5'9"; 165 pounds; excellent health; single; 22 years old

EDUCATION
Bachelor of Science, Marketing, expected June 1978

Marketing Courses	Background Courses
Marketing Seminar	Oral Communication
Sales Psychology	Psychology
Market Research	Economic Systems
Salesmanship	Food Chemistry
Sales Management	Report Writing
Retailing	Courses in Humanities

EXTRACURRICULAR
President of Senior Class; President of Sales Club; Member of Triad League, honorary marketing society; Winner of Bourke Cochran Public Speaking Contest 1975.

EXPERIENCE
Five years' experience, part-time and summers with A&P Supermarket, Ainsworthy Township, Texas, starting in junior year of high school. Stocked shelves and served as cashier.

One year experience, part-time and summer with Great Texas Food Mart in Great Texas Department Store, Brownsville. Supervisor of evening shelf stocking.

BACKGROUND
Born and raised in Texas; father a veterinarian. I have three older brothers, one a veterinarian and two in banking.

HOBBY
Food chemistry. Read widely on food processing. Have visited many canneries, bakeries, breweries, and food-packing companies in southern United States.

REFERENCES
Full references will be forwarded on request.

SALES REPRESENTATIVE

ARTHUR A. CRANDON

> 67 Fairview Boulevard
> Kilmarnock
> Michigan 87654

E N T E R P R I S I N G
P R O F E S S I O N A L
S A L E S
R E P R E S E N T A T I O N

JOB OBJECTIVE: To sell sophisticated products to professional buyers--
physicians, scientists, and educators.

RECORD OF ENTERPRISING SALES ACHIEVEMENT

> Pharmaceutical Salesman, Zermatt Corporation, Winchester,
> Michigan, 1975-Present.

- Call upon physicians in the city of Detroit, averaging
  eight to ten calls a day, displaying and explaining new
  products, and answering all questions, or getting answers
  to these questions from the home office.

- Keep myself knowledgeable on 1,000 products of the Zermatt
  line.

Desire change because career advancement opportunities are
limited at this moment in this company.

> College Textbook Salesman, Parkside-Robbins Publishing Company,
> Boston, Massachusetts, 1972-1975.

- Displayed catalogue of titles and promotional materials to
  department heads and professors in all colleges in the state
  of Connecticut, answering questions and urging adoptions.

- Solicited manuscripts for new textbooks.

During my three years with Parkside-Robbins, sales in the state
of Connecticut increased 25% each year. I left because Zermatt
offered a high salary with opportunity to advance to sales
manager.

EDUCATION

> Bachelor of Arts, Liberal Arts, Princeton University, 1972.
> Strong background in humanities with all electives in chemistry.

PERSONAL

> 28 years old; good appearance; father a surgeon; married;
> excellent health; six foot tall; 180 pounds.

REFERENCES

> Full references will be furnished on request.

MARY RAFFERTY

209 Van Buskirk Street
Queens Village
New York 09876
(212) 456 7890

EXECUTIVE

SECRETARY

Born June 23, 1943; 5'7", 124 pounds; excellent health; single

OBJECTIVE: To serve as executive secretary to first- or second-
echelon officer of major corporation.

SUMMARY: Seventeen years' experience as secretary, fourteen of
these with top corporate executives. Poised,
resourceful, excellent letter and report writer.
Excellent recommendations and references.

EXPERIENCE: Executive secretary and administrative assistant,
executive office, Atlantic Coast Building, Inc.,
New York City.

1969-   This large manufacturer of building materials with 15,000
Present employees has been purchased by International Plastics;
executive office being phased out.

Hired as secretary to president; placed in charge of
executive-office clerical staff (15 employees) when
president given additional assignment of board chairman.

Serve as administrative assistant to president; set up
all board and executive staff meetings, preparing agenda
and covering minutes; assist in preparation of all major
reports and directives issued by executive office;
prepare routine correspondence for signature of
president; supervise clerical staff.

1967-   Executive secretary to president, Boyden Steel
1969   Corporation, New York City. Assisted the president of
this large corporation (30,000 employees) in his
administrative duties; arranged meetings and trips; wrote
for his signature all routine letters and reports; and
maintained his office in his absence.

1964-   Secretary to sales staff, Tsarina Fabrics, New York City.
1967   Served staff of five textile salesmen writing
correspondence and typing records.

EDUCATION: Attended basic and advanced executive secretarial one-
week seminars of American Management Association, New
York City, 1972 and 1974.

Graduate of Julia Richman High School, New York City,
1964. Valedictorian of class.

REFERENCES: References will be forwarded on request.

John S. Levine

EXPERIENCED SECURITY DIRECTOR . . . RETIRED DETECTIVE

356 Arlington Street
Arlington, Virginia
09876
(123) 456 7890

53 years old
Excellent health
Married, sons adults
6'2", 195 pounds

OBJECTIVE   To provide security leadership and professional
             investigative services in department store, bank,
             stockbrokerage house, or plant, requiring policing,
             surveillance, and undercover investigations.

EXPERIENCE   Assistant Director of Security, Patoma Warehouse
             Corporation, Washington, D.C. 1968-Present.

             Assign guard personnel to 4 PM to midnight and midnight
             to 8 AM shifts, rotating 45 uniformed guards on full-
             shift and split-shift patrols.

             Investigate fires, thefts, frauds, and other problems
             involving security.

             Train all warehouse personnel in basic security.

             Detective (retired with rank of sergeant), New York City
             Police Department. 1947-1968.

             Excellent police record, cited five times for
             investigations. Accepted early retirement when wounded
             in line of duty; now fully recovered.

MILITARY   Sergeant, Military Police, United States Army, 1948-1951
             (on leave from New York City Police Department). Served
             in Hawaii.

EDUCATION   Graduate of Bryant High School, Queens, NYC; Delahanty
             Institute; and New York Police Academy.

REFERENCES   Full references will be furnished on request. Management
             of Patoma Warehouse knows of my desire to become a top
             security officer in some organization.

SOCIAL WORKER

PROFESSIONAL EXPERIENCE AND TRAINING OF AMY JONES, SOCIAL WORKER

45 Bank Street, Yonkers, New York; (213) 445 6789

Personal

Date of Birth: March 17, 1945   Height and Weight: 5'5"; 123 pounds

Place of Birth: Union, N.J.   Health: Excellent, no physical
                                             defects

Background: Father a physician   Marital Status: Single

Experience in Social Work

1975-present   Family Caseworker, Nondenominational Charities, Inc.,
                Yonkers, N.Y. Interviewed members of families at
                Nondenominational Hospital or at their homes,
                investigated needs, proposed plans for assistance,
                followed up on assistance offered.

1973-1975   Medical Caseworker, Paterson County Department of
                Hospitals, Paradise Valley, N.J. Interviewed families
                of patients to determine financial competence, arranged
                structure of fees to be paid by family, arranged for
                outpatient follow-up, counseled families for
                outpatient and convalescent cooperation.

Education

1969-1973   Bachelor of Science, Social Work, Manhattan University
                School of Social Work. Concentrated training in all
                areas of social work with varied short internships in
                pediatric, psychiatric, and rehabilitation areas.

1967-1969   Registered Nurse, Paterson County Hospital, Paradise
                Valley, New Jersey. Full training in all phases of
                general nursing, with special course in psychiatric
                nursing. Realized from experience that true interest
                lies in social work.

Professional Affiliations

National Association of Social Workers and Medical Caseworkers Society

Interests

Languages. Have good conversational and reading command of Spanish
and Italian. Good reading knowledge of French and German with fair
conversational ability. Travel to Puerto Rico and Mexico often to
improve and maintain Spanish.

References

References covering all phases of education and experience on request.

PROFESSIONAL QUALIFICATIONS OF JOHN C. MISPATT

FOR

APPOINTMENT AS SUPERINTENDENT OF SCHOOLS

536 Carroll Avenue, Wheaton, Indiana 98765, (203) 344-9211

Personal

General	Physical

<table>
<tr><td>Raised in Ames, Iowa</td><td>Born June 23, 1935</td></tr>
<tr><td>Married, three sons</td><td>Height 5'11"</td></tr>
<tr><td>Wife, BS, Iowa State</td><td>Weight 170 pounds</td></tr>
<tr><td>U.S. Army Veteran</td><td>Health excellent</td></tr>
</table>

Objective

Educator with Doctor of Education degree and twenty years'
experience, mainly as administrator, seeks appointment as
superintendent of schools in community desiring sensitive
leadership and quality education. Excellent record in
upgrading educational programs in accordance with wishes
of heterogeneous community.

Experience

Experience in School Administration

Acting Superintendent of Schools, Wheaton, Indiana,
1976-Present. Appointed to fill post during the leave of
absence of incumbent superintendent. Complete charge of
seven grade schools, one junior high school, and one senior
high. Commended for performance and offered position of
assistant superintendent upon return of the superintendent.
Prefer to seek a superintendent's post of my own.

Principal, Wheaton Senior High School, Wheaton, Indiana,
1970-present. (On leave from principal position while
serving as Acting Superintendent.) Wheaton High School has
faculty of 35 teachers, covering tenth, eleventh, and twelfth
grades for 900 students. Reorganized school curriculum in
1966 to reflect wishes of the first elected school board
of Wheaton. Hired one-third of the present faculty.
Evaluate all teachers for performance and sensitivity to
needs of minority groups. Established remedial programs for
disadvantaged students aspiring to college admission.

Vice Principal, Irvington High School, Irvington, Indiana,
1965-1970. This school has 50 teachers serving 1000
students. Evaluated teachers, planned curriculum, supervised
staff in principal's office, and established intramural
sports program. Reported to principal and filled in as
acting principal during his absence. Left to become
principal at Wheaton.

Experience in Teaching

English Teacher, Irvington High School, Irvington, Indiana,
1962-1965. Taught all four levels in a standard English
program. Served as dramatic coach and advisor to both
yearbook and newspaper. Promoted to position of vice
principal in 1965.

Remedial English Teacher, Irvington Public School System,
Irvington, Indiana, 1959-1962. As background for my doctoral
dissertation, I took this position in a program for the
disadvantaged. I designed a program in remedial English for
Irvington as part of my doctoral project. Although I had
intended to leave Irvington after gaining my degree, I was
persuaded to take post as English teacher in standard
program.

Education

Doctor of Education (Ed.D.). State University of Chicago,
Chicago, Illinois, 1964, Thesis: "English for the
Disadvantaged in a Heterogeneous Suburban School System."
My specialization in education for the disadvantaged gave me
both the insight and sensitivity that made possible my rapid
promotion in the Metropolitan Chicago Area.

Master of Arts (MA). State University of Chicago, Chicago,
Illinois, 1972. Thesis: "Social Problems Implied in
Chaucer."

Bachelor of Arts (BA). University of Iowa, Iowa City, Iowa,
1957. Majored in English and minored in economics.

Military

Major, US Army, served in West Germany, 1957-1959.

Interests

My wife and I share an intense interest in the Wheaton
Community Players. We stage shows in the Chicago Area.
My three sons have performed in these shows.

SWITCHBOARD OPERATOR

Marilyn Brown

4125 Millville Street
St. Paul, Minnesota 09876
(123) 456 9876

---

all models	SWITCHBOARD OPERATOR	pleasant manner

personal   32 years old; excellent health; 5'6", 119 pounds; single.

experience   fifteen years switchboard experience, including reception and typing; earlier typing and sales experience.

1974-date ● **Lutetia Fabrics, Inc., St. Paul**

      high-fashion dress manufacturer, employs 875; currently operate 608-A two-position board; have operated 555 and 608 in Minneapolis sales office; also type and serve as receptionist.

      firm moving to Chicago.

1972-1974 ● **Minneapolis Mills, Inc., Minneapolis**

      major cereal manufacturer, employs 15,000; operated 556 board; served as receptionist; typed sales reports.

1964-1972 ● **Minneapolis Mart, Minneapolis**

      supervised and operated various positions on main board from 1966 to 1972, when this large department store went out of business.

      served as typist, salesgirl, and wrapper from 1964 to 1966.

education   graduate of Minneapolis Central High School, commercial course, June, 1964. honor grades in typing, office practice, business English, and commercial arithmetic. won two national typing awards.

hobbies   tennis, golf, and reading.

references   references will be forwarded on request.

MAIN QUALIFICATIONS OF DOLORES KAY SYLVESTER

45 Pell Street
Upper Montclair
New Jersey 07004
(201) 234 5578

Management Systems Analyst

Seven years of high-level systems design experience.

Five years of sophisticated computer programming
experience.

Master of Business Administration, San Francisco
University.

Bachelor of Science in Electrical Engineering, San
Francisco University.

34 years old, single, ready to locate in any part of
world. Fluent command of Spanish. Natural-born
United States citizen.

FULL RESUME WILL BE FORWARDED ON REQUEST.

A synopsis (qualification) resume is mailed to screen
prospects. If response is gained, a fuller resume like one
on following page is sent to prospect. See discussion of
synopsis resume on pages 153-154.

DOLORES KAY SYLVESTER

Management Systems Analyst with Strong Large-Computer Experience

45 Pell Street
Upper Montclair
New Jersey 07004
(201) 234 5578

34 years old
Single, (Can Relocate)
Excellent health
5'6", 130 pounds

OBJECTIVE: To serve as senior systems analyst in computer
center of large corporation where my knowledge
of sophisticated systems procedures and CPM/PERT
can be applied to challenging problems.

EXPERIENCE

1975-
Present

Three years of high-level systems design experience with
TREMONT, BERKLEY, AND SANDS, New York City, one of
the nation's largest management consulting firms, as
Manager, Systems Design.

● Consulted with clients, reviewed problems and
developed proposals, specifying phase by phase an
engagement to utilize present hardware or to purchase
(or rent) advanced hardware, to design and install
sophisticated system, and to implement installation
and initial operation of new system, including
orientation of personnel.

● Developed and implemented systems designs and
programs as contracted with clients, consulting with
senior management of client on gross systems design
and subsystems design, recommending computers,
developing objectives and constraints, and building
mathematical models and programs.

Desire change because interested in career with a
larger corporation.

1973-
1975

Two years of solid systems design experience with
INTERNATIONAL AIRCRAFT, INC., Los Angeles, a
medium-sized, but important, aircraft manufacturer.

● Developed logic design for digital computers and
peripheral equipment.

● Designed accounting system to integrate with total
management system.

1968-
1973

Five years' experience in computer programming with
SIMONS FALLS INSURANCE COMPANY, Simons Falls,
Washington. Worked with systems analyst
standardizing all accounting, billing, purchasing,
and policy management in a single system, developing
all programs.

EDUCATION   Master of Business Administration (MBA), Accounting,
                       SCHOOL OF BUSINESS, SAN FRANCISCO UNIVERSITY.
1967-   Thesis: "Computer Science Applications of
1968   Accounting in Five American Corporations."

                   Bachelor of Science in Electrical Engineering (BSEE)
1962-   (five year course), COLLEGE OF ENGINEERING, SAN
1967   FRANCISCO UNIVERSITY. Full training in electrical
                   engineering with heavy minor in mathematics. Learned
                   mathematical model building in a pioneering course
                   that anticipated total systems approach to computer
                   design. Graduated Summa Cum Laude.

BACKGROUND   Born in Oakland, California; attended Oakland schools,
                       except for five years' residence in Venezuela where
                       father served as engineer with oil company; mother
                       taught mathematics in Oakland and Caracas; speak and
                       write Spanish fluently; lifelong interest in
                       mathematics.

AFFILIATIONS   Member of three major professional societies:

                   ● National Society for Systems Analysts

                   ● American Association of Electrical Engineers

                   ● American Association of Computer Scientists

INTERESTS   Ballet; opera; philosophy, particularly ontology

REFERENCES   Mr. Raymond Jankowitz, Partner in Charge of Management
                       Consulting, Tremont, Berkley, and Sands, 490 Madison
                       Avenue, New York City 10032

                   Mr. Salvatore Lamonte, President, International
                       Aircraft, Inc., 567 Oriente Boulevard, Los
                       Angeles 90003

                   Mr. Arthur Simonelli, Director, Computer Center, Simons
                       Falls Insurance Company, Simons Falls, Washington

                   Dean Ralph C. Saunders, School of Business, San
                       Francisco University, San Francisco

TECHNICAL WRITER

EXPERIENCED TECHNICAL WRITER AND EDITOR WITH ENGINEERING DEGREE

AND PROVEN COPY RECORD AVAILABLE FOR PRODUCTIVE PERFORMANCE

Brian Costello

35 White Plains Avenue
Candlewood, N.Y. 10707
(914) 337-0987

Personal

28 Years Old
Married, One Child
Excellent Health

---TECHNICAL WRITING AND EDITING EXPERIENCE---

Eight years' heavy technical writing and editing experience with
electronics manufacturer and with engineering company.

● Technical Editor, ELECTRO-TEL SYSTEMS, INC., La Jolla, California
(1974-Present). Led editorial staff of ten technical writers and
production personnel. Supervised production of technical manuals,
brochures, bulletins, and specification sheets. Conferred with
electronic designers, minicomputer technicians, and marketing
specialists assisting in component design as well as writing
technical copy. Developed both technical copy and interpretive
copy that simplified digital and electronic applications.

● Technical Writer, DRANFORTH ENGINEERING CO., Dranforth, New York
(1972-1974). Prepared technical bulletins and technical
advertising. Helped engineering staff prepare proposals and
presentations. Surveyed clients' needs and personnel technical
comprehension and developed literature, correspondence, and
reports interpreting engineering projects.

---TECHNICAL EDUCATION---

Combined engineering baccalaureate with certificate in journalism and
technical writing.

● Certificate in Journalism, PROFESSIONAL BUSINESS AND TECHNICAL
WRITERS SCHOOL OF MANHATTAN, New York. (1972-1973).

● Bachelor of Science, Mechanical Engineering, LAFAYETTE COLLEGE,
Easton, Pennsylvania (1968-1972). Complete training in basic
engineering. Served as editor of college newspaper.

---REFERENCES---

References and other documentation testifying to strong track record
will be furnished on request.

TOOL AND DIE MAKER

RALPH P. PETRONOV   First Class

63 Fremont Avenue   T O O L   A N D   D I E   M A K E R
Erie, New York 09876
(123) 456 7890

42 years old; married, adult son; excellent health; 6', 180 pounds

> Objective: To serve as foreman or as tool designer
> in top-notch tool shop or in tool and die department
> of heavy equipment manufacturer.

Experience

Twenty-two years' experience in tool and die making and in tool design.

TOOL DESIGNER   ACE TRUCK & TRAILER COMPANY
  1973-Date   Rochester, New York

> Design all tools, dies, jigs, fixtures, gauges, and
> special parts needed in the manufacture of truck bodies,
> trailers, plows, and farm machinery. Supervise the
> work of five tool and die makers, two apprentices,
> three laborers. Confer with engineers and production
> superintendent, develop blueprints, oversee production,
> and check feasibility. Serve as advisor to machine
> shop foreman. Company relocating to Kentucky.

TOOL AND DIE MAKER   TRI-STATE TOOL AND DIE SHOP
  1958-1973   Rochester, New York

> Prepared all tools and dies needed in Rochester
> industrial plants. Worked closely with design
> engineer of automobile body manufacturer learning
> advanced tool design, blueprinting, and engineering
> mathematics. Hold patents on devices used in the
> stamping department of auto body manufacturers.

Education and Apprenticeship

Four-year apprenticeship in Tri-State Tool and Die shop, 1954-1958.

Graduate of Rochester Trade School (three-year course), 1951-1954.

References

Mr. Albert Goldsmith, Vice President, Rochester Niagara National Bank,
  76 Genessee Street, Rochester, New York.

Mr. Philip Adler, President, Ace Truck & Trailer Company, 45 Rail
  Street, Rochester, New York.

Mr. Al Thompson, Proprietor, Tri-State Tool and Die Shop, 14 Mill
  Street, Rochester, New York.

TRAINING SUPERVISOR

THOMAS R. LARSEN

Training Supervisor and Employee Development Specialist

56 Palisades Boulevard   Born April 1, 1946
Englewood Cliffs   6'2", 195 pounds
New Jersey 09876   Excellent health
(201) 543 8967   Married, one child

OBJECTIVE: To serve as training director and help build an
employee development center in large corporation
needing extensive staff development

EXPERIENCE

Training Coordinator, Metropolitan National Bank, New York City,
1971-Present. Helped organize the training department of this
large bank, designing and programming courses, interviewing
teaching and technical staff. Launched rehabilitation program for
dropouts and hard-core unemployed.

Assist in administration	Confer with training director in designing courses, buying equipment, and managing staff of 26. Help establish standards for teaching personnel.
Develop programmed courses	Survey teaching equipment market for cassette courses, programmed courses, and teaching aids that can be adapted to our needs. Write teaching manuals and help develop courses on tape recorders and transparencies.
Supervise opportunity program	Serve as director of opportunity program which I launched, hire teachers, select aids, and design courses in English, mathematics, and bank skills.

Staff Instructor. LaGuardia Life Insurance Company, New York City,
1969-1971. Taught courses in supervisory and executive skills,
communication, and employee relations.

Instructor in Industrial Psychology. Stuyvesant Junior College, New
York, 1968-1969.

EDUCATION

Master of Arts, Psychology, Graduate School of Arts and Sciences,
MacDougal University, Ottawa, Canada, 1968.

Bachelor of Science, Business Education, Montclair State College,
Montclair, New Jersey, 1967.

REFERENCES

References will be furnished on request.

UNDERWRITER TRAINEE

RAYMOND D. SHELL
UNDERWRITER TRAINEE

44 Roman Boulevard, Afton City, Tennessee 37616 (615) 742-9812

PERSONAL

Born March 9, 1953 in Afton City, Tennessee   Health: Excellent
Grew up in Afton City area   Height: 5'11"
Military Status: Separated, Army, 1st Lt.   Weight: 180 lbs.
Marital Status: Single

EDUCATION

Heston University, Tremont, Tennessee
Bachelor of Science in Marketing, June, 1980, in curriculum that
included:

Marketing Courses	Background Courses
Marketing Management	Business Report Writing
Consumer Analysis	Economics I & II
Retail Management	Principles of Management
Marketing Logistics	Principles of Accounting I & II
Advertising and Promotion	Theory of Money and Credit
Public Relations	Journalistic Writing
Market Research	Statistics

EXPERIENCE

Part-Time and Summer Experience

Triangle Candy Distributors, 3 summers, 1977, 1978, 1979, Milton
City, Tennessee.

Main duties:

Worked in warehouse storing boxes of candy
Mailed promotional posters to supermarkets
Recorded bills for accountant and performed
other clerical duties

Military

Supply Officer (6 months-Fort Dix)   Company Commander (3 months-
Club Officer (3 months-Fort Bragg)   Fort Dix)
Company Commander (6 months-Fort   Military Instructor
  Bragg)   (3 months-Fort Riley)
                Separation Officer
                  (3 months-Fort Riley)

EXTRACURRICULAR ACTIVITIES

Heston University: Community:
President: Market Club (Senior year)   Member: Heston Social Club
Member: Ski Club (Junior & Senior years)   President: Afton Investors'
Member: Stock Market Club (Senior year)   Club

REFERENCES

Prof. Margaret Keller, Marketing Department, Heston University
Mr. Mark P. Zelder, Manager, Triangle Candy Distributors, Milton City,
Tennessee

WORD PROCESSOR

LIOBA ECCLES

45 Santiago Place
Scottsdale, Arizona 85483
(435) 365-1098

WORD

PROCESSOR

Excellent Health; 5'6", 125 lbs.; 25 years old; Single

WORD PROCESSOR with eight years' responsible word-processing experience, trained in both IBM and Redactron systems, with knowledge of components and applications, seeks advanced position in word processing with major Sunbelt corporation.

WORD-PROCESSING EXPERIENCE

Supervisor, Word-Processing Unit, ZUNI-MESA INSURANCE, INC., Phoenix, Arizona, (1974-Present).

- Participated in the survey, planning, and implementing of Zuni-Mesa office automation. Applied Redactron Advice-and-Counsel Survey Kit to old office procedures. Conferred with Data-Processing Manager of Zuni-Mesa and Burroughs Branch Manager on word-processing needs of new system.

- Began as operator of dual-card text editor and advanced to present supervisory position. Helped develop and train operators for Redactor-II Video Display System, the foundation of the Zuni-Mesa high-throughput Processing Center.

Operator, IBM, MTST, CAMELBACK INDUSTRIES, Scottsdale, Arizona, (1972-1974). Selected for position from typing pool as first word processor in firm.

EDUCATION

Graduate of Phoenix High School (1972) and Scottsdale Business College (1974). Learned word processing in intensive in-house programs conducted by IBM (April, 1973) and Burroughs (August, 1975).

REFERENCES

Present employer knows of desire to serve multimillion dollar corporation with sophisticated word-processing system encompassing data storage and national communication. Will furnish full references on request.

SECTION 2

GETTING READY TO WRITE YOUR RESUME

HAVE YOUR FACTS READY

An effective resume is built from carefully chosen data. Some of this data appears in school catalogues, course reports, work schedules, and letters. The best of it, however, is generally locked in your mind and must be drawn forth through scratch-pad analysis. An important preliminary to resume writing is the gathering and processing of the data needed for your resume.

> ### TIP
> Gather career data before you write your resume.

If you do not have at your fingertips all your career data, you will have difficulty selecting the resume design best for you. As you write your resume, you may omit items that do not come to mind. You may be vague in areas where you could be specific.

GATHERING PERSONAL RECORDS

Have ready the dates, school courses, past jobs, and other specific facts you need for your resume. Locate that high school or college yearbook, that school catalogue, that military certificate of services, that school transcript, that letter of commendation, those newspaper clippings about you, and any other documents that yield the facts you need. Make a few telephone calls to recover details you do not have on record.

> ### TIP
> Have available specific details you need to give your resume authority.

Vagueness is the greatest single weakness found in most resumes. Do all the preliminary legwork necessary to gain concrete specific data.

SUPPLEMENTING AND INTERPRETING PERSONAL RECORDS

Generally, your personal records need supplementing and interpreting. You may find that some of your documents fail to provide the full picture.

For example: That course in general science may have been given by a professor of geology who conducted field trips to a nearby mountain on Sunday afternoons. That job of bookkeeper may have included considerable payroll preparation. That hitch in the army may have included advanced training in conversational German. Facts like these should be added to your personal records. You may need these facts when you compose your resume.

Often your personal records need interpreting. You interpret facts when you comment on the meaning and importance of an experience. Consider a young man who feels that a course entitled *Oral Communication* was the most valuable he took in college. Examining his college catalogue, he reads the following entry for this course:

> Speech 3, Oral Communication, T-T, 1-3, F-S, 9-11.
> Inculcates knowledge of and skill in basic speech media including interviews, conferences, and platform presentations. Lecture supplemented by practice sessions. Prerequisite English 1 and 2. Six points.

Then examining his college transcript, he finds the dates when he took the course and the grade received.

These facts are important but they do not reveal the true meaning of the course to him. Actually, this course contributed substantially to his chosen career—Public Relations. Thinking about *Oral Communication* for a moment, he writes the following interpretive note:

> INTERPRETATIVE NOTE
>
> Actually a basic public speaking course, Oral Communication showed me that I command an important PR skill. A PR man must be a good oral communicator. My A in every presentation testified to this skill. Particularly helpful were the video screenings of my presentations and the comments of the instructor. Not only did I learn techniques for interviewing and holding conferences, but I learned how to use my personality to make audiences like me, believe me, and accept my ideas. This course helped me relate the principles I learned in written communication to oral presentations, and both these skills contribute to my career goal in public relations.

Consider the young woman who took a statistics course evenings in an insurance school. Reviewing a brochure on the course, she found the following description of the course:

> BROCHURE STATEMENT
>
> *Introduction to Statistics.* Covers measurement of central tendency, probability, and analysis needed for business decisions. Students who enroll must have a working knowledge of high school algebra.

Asking herself the question: "What does this course mean to me in terms of an insurance career? " she wrote:

Consider the young woman who reviewed her experience as a biochemistry aide with a university. Examining her records she found the following official statements:

Asking herself the question: "What did I really achieve on this job?," she wrote:

It is especially important to interpret military, marine corps, air force, and naval experiences into civilian life counterparts. Note how the military experiences to the left in the following table have the civilian life equivalents listed in the column to the right.

Military Occupation	Civilian Equivalent
Supply Sergeant	Warehouse Manager
Captain in Charge of Motor Pool	Traffic Manager
Naval Communication Officer	Telephone Company District Manager
Company Clerk	Personnel Specialist
Sergeant, Military Police	Security Manager

DECIDING JOB AND CAREER OBJECTIVES

One of the most important items you can develop is your job objective.

TIP
Write your job objective in a single sentence.

Effective resumes are always built foursquare upon a specific job objective.

Importance of a Job Objective

Having a specific job goal gives you purpose and confidence in the job campaign. You are hired to solve specific problems. Never think, feel, say, or write: "I'm applying for anything open," "I'm willing to do anything," or "I'm leaving things like careers wide open." These statements show indecision, immaturity, and unemployability.

Having specific job goals and long-range objectives provides you with a basis for building your resume. Note how all the "Job-Getting Resumes" of Section 1 are built upon specific job goals. If you qualify for two different job goals, prepare a separate resume for each of these goals.

"Know Thyself—Know Thy Work"

The successful careerist works constantly with two precepts:

Know yourself!

Know your work!

The best way to know yourself and know your work is very simple:

Ask yourself!

Write two basic questions on a sheet of paper, allowing yourself room for answers to each question.

What is (are) my immediate job goal(s)?

What is my long-range job objective?

Can you supply an instant answer to each of these important questions?

If you are experienced—say, an accountant or a restaurant manager—and happy in your line, you may have no trouble with either question.

ACCOUNTANT:

> #### What are my immediate job goals?
>
> I want a position as a tax accountant with a certified public accounting firm.
>
> #### What is my long-range objective?
>
> Eventually, I want to become a partner in a certified public accounting firm.

RESTAURANT MANAGER:

> #### What are my immediate job goals?
>
> I want a position as a manager or assistant manager of a restaurant in a large restaurant or hotel chain.
>
> #### What is my long-range objective?
>
> I want an executive position with a large restaurant or hotel chain.

"Ask Thyself"

If you can't answer these two basic questions instantly, you must probe your mind deeper.

TIP

Probe your mind through scratch-pad analysis whenever you need deep insight to your personal preferences.

Write questions like these on separate sheets of paper:

> (1) What would I like most to do in life?

> (2) What satisfactions have I gained from past experiences and what kind of work provides these satisfactions?

> (3) What goal is indicated by my present record of training and experience?

Consider for example, Question 1, *What would I like most to do in life?* Write the question at the head of your scratch paper. Have about six or seven extra blank sheets ready for capturing your full response.

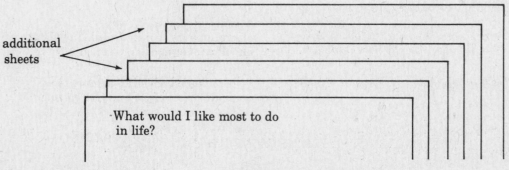

additional sheets

What would I like most to do in life?

115

Read the question aloud. Job titles should spring to mind—say, *bank employee* or *travel agent*. Write down these job titles, but leave space for later comments of the mind.

If no job titles come to mind, relax and wait. Perhaps you are pressing too hard. Or perhaps you are overcritical of the job titles the mind does offer. Be patient and accept uncritically any titles the mind offers. Your immediate objective is to get job titles flowing.

The chances are strong that two or three job titles will crowd into your mind at the same time—say, *bank employee, real estate agent, travel agent*. The minute you write down *bank employee,* three more titles may rush to mind—say, *traveling representative, accountant* and *internal auditor*. Get all these titles down; they are all valuable. But space them out. Remember, you need room also for the comments that your mind delivers about each job title.

If you are a teenager, or in your early twenties, the entry *bank employee* and the comments your mind offers might appear:

Job title that springs to mind	Feelings and comments that spring to mind

Bank Employee

I've always liked banks ... when I was in grammar school I thought working in a bank was the best kind of job to have.	I'm quick at figures ... I like to talk to people ... If I worked for one of the banks in my city, the bank would pay my tuition at night college.
Bank work is clean, respected work.	Bank work is good. It's steady work.

Banks are good for communities. A merchant once told me that banks really make a city prosper.

I must consider this work seriously—the bankers I know are the most respected people in town.

JOB TITLE AND REACTIONS OF A TEENAGE APPLICANT

If you are older and more experienced, the job title and the comments your mind offers might appear:

Job title that springs to mind	Feelings and comments that spring to mind

Bank Employee

With decreasing opportunity in investment houses, I might be wise to apply at banks. Maybe the personal trust or corporate trust department of a large city bank would be interested in me.	Actually, I considered banking when I first came out of school. Even when I was advancing in that stockbrokerage firm, I considered switching to some bank.
I certainly know a lot about investments and I would be valuable to a bank.	I could also qualify very well for the operations division of a bank. I'm good at office management, including purchasing.
I can see myself working for a bank.	I have a good friend in a savings and loan association ... I might consider savings and loan work. It's like banking.

JOB TITLE AND REACTIONS OF AN EXPERIENCED APPLICANT

Imagine that *travel agent* springs next to mind.

If you are a teenager, the entry *travel agent* and the comments your mind offers might appear:

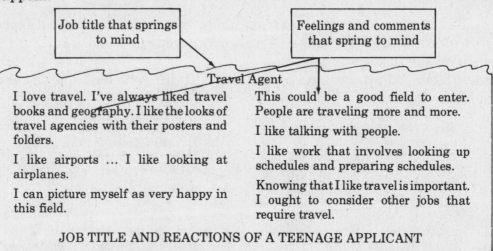

| Job title that springs to mind | Feelings and comments that spring to mind |

Travel Agent

I love travel. I've always liked travel books and geography. I like the looks of travel agencies with their posters and folders.

I like airports ... I like looking at airplanes.

I can picture myself as very happy in this field.

This could be a good field to enter. People are traveling more and more.

I like talking with people.

I like work that involves looking up schedules and preparing schedules.

Knowing that I like travel is important. I ought to consider other jobs that require travel.

JOB TITLE AND REACTIONS OF A TEENAGE APPLICANT

If you are an older, experienced applicant, the entry *travel agent* and your comments of mind might appear:

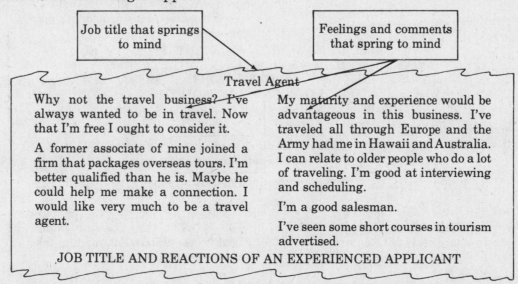

| Job title that springs to mind | Feelings and comments that spring to mind |

Travel Agent

Why not the travel business? I've always wanted to be in travel. Now that I'm free I ought to consider it.

A former associate of mine joined a firm that packages overseas tours. I'm better qualified than he is. Maybe he could help me make a connection. I would like very much to be a travel agent.

My maturity and experience would be advantageous in this business. I've traveled all through Europe and the Army had me in Hawaii and Australia. I can relate to older people who do a lot of traveling. I'm good at interviewing and scheduling.

I'm a good salesman.

I've seen some short courses in tourism advertised.

JOB TITLE AND REACTIONS OF AN EXPERIENCED APPLICANT

If you devote several probing sessions to Question 1 over a period of three or four days, you will accumulate a number of highly indicative job titles and some very valuable comments on the kinds of work you really want to do. Spread these comments on the table and read them thoughtfully. They will spell out clearly the areas where your true interests lie. Put them aside for later reference.

Now try Question 2.

What satisfactions have I gained from past experiences and what kinds of work provide these satisfactions?

Read the question aloud. Memories of past satisfactions should take form in your mind—*the thrill of making a sale, the delight of creating something or building something, the glow of being outdoors, the excitement of lively people around me, being in the midst of action, the satisfaction of writing a story,* or *the fulfillment I get when I lead a group.*

Write these satisfactions down as they come to mind. Identify the past experiences that gave you these satisfactions. If a job occurs to you that could provide one of these satisfactions, jot down that job title.

Your scratch-pad analysis might take several different forms as the examples which follow indicate:

Desired satisfaction that springs to mind	Comments on that satisfaction

Being in the Midst of Excitement

Liked the liveliness when I worked in a department store ... loved the constant parade of people ... the crowds at sale ... the hours were long but the time went fast.

Liked restaurant work and hotel work ... liked ushering.

Like the crowds, noise, and fun at school carnivals ... I was great as a barker for the sideshow ... I like visiting carnivals, circuses, and amusement parks.

I like anything with a lot of people around ... When I worked for the electronic supply house the boss said I was good because excitement didn't upset me.

BANK TELLER...BANQUET ASSISTANT IN A HOTEL DEPARTMENT STORE SALESMAN ... ENTERTAINMENT ... FASHION DISPLAY ... HOTEL WORK ... RESTAURANT WORK ... MERCHANDISING ... PROMOTION ... CONVENTION WORK.

Title of jobs that might provide that satisfaction

SATISFACTION DESIRED AND REACTIONS OF A TEENAGE APPLICANT

SATISFACTION: *Glow of outdoor life.* In many years of construction work, I like being outdoors more than anything else.

SATISFACTION: *Building things.* Love to see things I'm building take shape—especially homes.

POSSIBLE JOBS

CONTINUE IN CONSTRUCTION ... START HOME IMPROVEMENT FIRM ... SELL HOME IMPROVEMENTS ... SELL REAL ESTATE ... START A FUEL BUSINESS IN MY HOME ... GET INTO BUILDING DEPARTMENT IN MY TOWN ... WORK FOR A HARDWARE DEALER ... SELL PREFAB HOMES ... WORK FOR A UTILITY COMPANY.

SATISFACTION: *Pride in working out mechanical problems.* Give me any mechanical problem whether it's a puzzle or house wiring and I'll solve it.

SATISFACTION: *Delight in dealing with people.* Get a kick out of dealing directly with people. My wife thinks I'm a natural salesman. As a matter of fact, I was great at door-to-door selling when I was a kid.

SATISFACTIONS DESIRED AND REACTIONS OF AN EXPERIENCED APPLICANT

118

Now try Question 3.

Question 3 lets your record speak, but it also involves your deeper processes of mind.

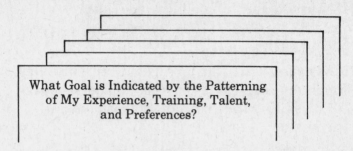

What Goal is Indicated by the Patterning of My Experience, Training, Talent, and Preferences?

Consider your schooling, your jobs, your hobbies, your travels, and your many other experiences. Ask yourself such questions as: Why did I major in architecture? Why did I take a job as a sales trainee? Why did I stay so long in that warehouse job? Why do I prefer books on rivers and lakes? Why do I always vacation in Yosemite? Why do I prefer Paris to other cities in Europe?

If you are in your teens or early twenties, these questions will reveal the kinds of satisfactions you habitually seek. Generally, you will see one pronounced pattern emerge—say, you like designing things, you like to make sales, or you have great intellectual curiosity.

If you are over thirty, these questions will help you pattern your training and experiences in terms of a solid job objective. When you design a resume, write an application letter, or conduct an interview, you want to present a view of achievements that move toward a goal. Probing for patterns will show you how your college major in architecture, your visit to great art galleries, your experience in package design, and your job as production editor of a trade journal all support your goal of becoming promotional director of a prefabricated home manufacturer.

JOB-MARKET FOCUS

You know yourself and know your work by asking yourself: *What would I like most to do in life?* Naturally, the jobs that spring to mind are jobs you have seen in action, jobs your friends and relatives hold, jobs you have heard about in conversations, books, or studies. The more jobs you know, the better your chances of selecting the right job objective.

Your job objective must be right for you, but it must also be realistic in terms of the job market. The job must exist and be available to you.

Self-analysis should always be accompanied by job-market surveys. If you are young, learn about all the different careers open to you. Your skill in mathematics may point to accounting, computer programming, or engineering because these are fields you know. But what about *insurance actuarial work?* Here is an excellent field for the superior mathematician, but few apply. Why? They don't know the attractive job opportunity exists.

If you are experienced, keep abreast of changes in the job market. Your years in industry may point to production jobs. But couldn't that earlier training in accounting be combined with your knowledge of industry and make you a first-rate *operational auditor?*

Talk to people. Ask questions about jobs. Browse through your library and look for job-market information. Read out-of-town newspapers, as well as your hometown paper. Read biographies. Read business and trade magazines, professional journals, house organs, and annual reports.

Your library carries standard directories that are indispensable in your job campaign—government directories like the *Dictionary of Occupational Titles* or business directories like *Moody's Industrial Manual.* Particularly valuable are Gertrude Forrester's *Occupational Literature* and the *College Placement Annual.* An annotated bibliography containing these and other valuable guides will be found in the Appendix of this book, beginning on page 190.

The staffs of employment agencies, executive recruiting companies, and placement bureaus are widely knowledgeable on the job market. Ask them questions about the job market and about specific occupations. "What does a fashion coordinator do?" "What is a manufacturer's representative?" "Is there much demand for manufacturer's representatives?"

Read want ads. Read the business sections of big-city newspapers like the *New York Times* and note the new high-demand occupations that are developing today: *electronic analyst, financial analyst, computer application specialist, microbiologist, designer of automatic machinery, hardware trader, biomedical abstractor, hotel marketing executive, copy supervisor,* and *nonferrous metal trader.*

MATCHING YOUR QUALIFICATIONS TO JOB-MARKET DEMAND

Self-inventories survey your qualifications. *Job-market reviews* apprise you of work opportunities. Your mind constantly balances your capabilities and desires against the opportunities and demands of the job market. If you probe your mind with scratch-pad analysis, you can usually gain a realistic job objective for your resume.

This automatic matching of your qualifications against the specifics of job-market demand generally needs some refining and reinforcement. Your resume is a precisely tuned instrument. You must know exactly how your qualifications match the demands of your job objective.

The technique of the balance sheet is very simple and most helpful. To prepare a balance sheet, you run a vertical line down the middle of a sheet of paper. You can judge your suitability for a certain career—say, department-store work or teaching—by matching your qualifications, item by item, with specific demands for that career. List on the left side of the sheet items of temperament, talent, education, and experience needed in that career. Try to match each of these demands by entering items of your temperament, talent, and education on the right side of the sheet.

When you view the specifics of your qualifications this way, you will see the practicality of your job objective, deficiencies you must overcome to attain that objective, and weaknesses you must bolster when you develop your resume.

Consider the advertising copywriter with agency experience who decided that his real career was in industry. Forming a job objective of working as manager of an advertising department in a manufacturing company, he tested his new objective on a balance sheet.

Dividing a worksheet with a vertical line, he listed job requirements as he found them in want ads and matched them item for item against his qualifications.

BALANCE SHEET OF ADVERTISING MANAGER

My Qualifications	Job Requirements
Eight years' agency experience.	Experienced advertising man with company or agency experience.
Direct knowledge of agencies, having worked for one.	Ability to deal with advertising agencies.
Skilled and experienced in both visualization and copywriting.	Visualization and writing skills.
Indirectly concerned with research *but minor in statistics gives me expert command of important research tool.*	Some experience in advertising research.

This balance sheet showed the applicant how his experience matched all but one of the job requirements. Fortunately, one item of his education compensated for this weakness in experience. Casting this balance sheet helped the applicant understand himself better and helped him adapt his data for use in his resume and covering letter.

Balance sheets have many uses in the preliminaries to resume writing. As illustrated, they align education, experience, and other qualifications to the specific demands of work sought. But they also serve as devices for measuring the *pros* and *cons* in critical career decisions.

For example, you can evaluate the advantages of taking employment in another part of the country or of changing your career by placing the *pros* (arguments for) in one column and *cons* (arguments against) in another.

Balance sheets are useful for weighing one alternative career against another.

For example, a home economics major found that she could not get a job teaching home economics because of a job shortage. She did have two excellent offerings: (1) to teach handicapped children and (2) to serve as a home economist with a food manufacturer. She set up a balance sheet as follows:

BALANCE SHEET OF HOME ECONOMIST

Give Up Home Economics To Teach Handicapped	Stay in Home Economics But Work in Industry
Fully qualified through courses in special education, as well as teaching license.	Fully qualified through training in home economics and ability to write letters and reports.
Moderate interest in teaching but like to help the young. I was so-so about practice teaching. This area would be especially rewarding to my conscience but as a martyr.	Little opportunity to teach, although teaching could be incidental part of this work.
Little opportunity to use knowledge of home economics, my true interest, although home economics could be incidental subject matter.	High interest in home economics. This job would offer more opportunity to practice sophisticated home economics than teaching. But home economics is very important to me.
Moderate pay with little opportunity to advance into high-pay area. Pay means little to me.	Higher pay with excellent opportunity to advance into high-pay areas—especially with my writing and administrative gifts. But pay not important to me.

Matching these critical items, this young woman made her decision very easily. Her knowledge of self gained through earlier scratch-pad analysis revealed that home economics meant much more to her than teaching. The idea of helping the handicapped appealed very strongly to her for humanitarian reasons. The idea of entering industry because it paid more caused her guilt. But this balance sheet showed her that she would probably do more harm than good if she had to give up home economics to enter teaching.

Balance sheets can be expanded into *decision tables*. Consider the applicant who had three courses open to him at age thirty-five. He could become a *systems analyst*, a *production manager*, or an *operational auditor*. To clarify the way, he cast a decision table in the following form.

DECISION TABLE FOR CHOICE OF CAREER

My Qualifications	Systems Analysis	Production Management	Operational Auditing
Item	Requirement	Requirement	Requirement
Item	Requirement	Requirement	Requirement
Item	Requirement	Requirement	Requirement
Item	Requirement	Requirement	Requirement

Viewing his qualifications in terms of three possible careers, the applicant saw in a glance that he was best suited in temperament, education, and experience to work as a systems analyst.

PROJECTING ALTERNATE CAREER COURSES IN A DECISION TREE

Sometimes the best way to judge alternate courses of action is to project them side by side in a decision tree.

Consider the young man or woman who must make the following career decision: *Should I accept the position offered by X Department Store to work as a sales clerk or the position offered by Y Bank to work as a general clerk?*

This applicant could project each possible career in a decision tree. Spreading a large piece of paper—say, one yard square—on the kitchen floor, the applicant could write the basic question in a box in the middle of the left edge of the sheet. With the question posed, he could draw one-year paths leading to the consequences of each career choice:

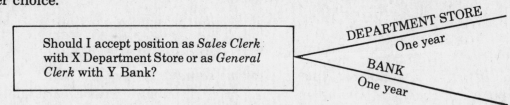

A little research would tell the applicant where he would be at the end of a year for each career choice. The department store choice could make him a junior manager of some section. The bank choice could make him a section head. The applicant could then project three-year paths. With these positions plotted, the applicant could project probable positions for five years later. This nine-year projection would pattern somewhat as follows.

A full illustration of a decision tree resolving this problem appears on page 189 of the Appendix.

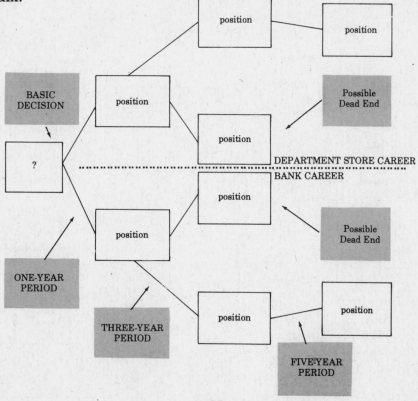

THE OCCUPATIONAL WORKSHEET

The last step in processing data for the resume is building an *occupational worksheet*.

An occupational worksheet (known also as a *career blueprint* or a *personal record sheet* or a *work qualification inventory)* is a private, unslanted, detailed summary of the data you need for information, guidance, and decisions in the job campaign. Two examples of occupational worksheets will be found on pages 179 through 188 in the Appendix of this book.

When you build an occupational worksheet, you pull together all of the data you have developed from your personal records, your self-analysis, and your job-market surveys.

The following diagram shows how the occupational worksheet (a) combines and organizes the key data of personal records, self-analysis, and job-market analysis, and (b) provides a basic record and guide for all steps in the job campaign.

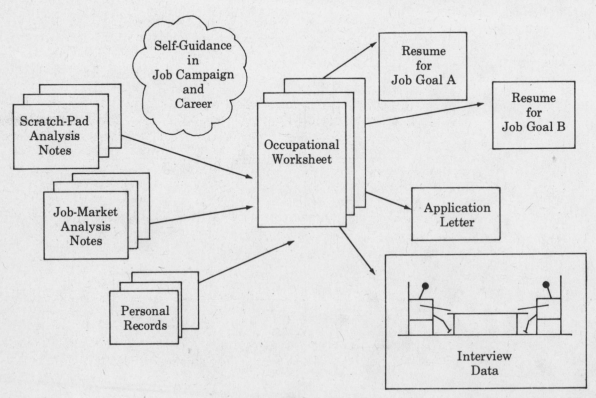

An occupational worksheet is easily built in two stages:

1. Drafting the Occupational Worksheet. Assemble your personal records and self-analysis notes and place them on your desk or somewhere near your desk. Take a pile of 8½-by-11-inch sheets or a legal pad and head each sheet with one of the following labels, a different heading on each sheet: *Personal Details, Job Goals and Long-Range Objectives, General Background, Career Timetable, Handicaps and Other Personal Limitations, Education and Training, Work History, Achievements, Special Talents, Military Service, Honors and Awards, Travel, Professional Societies, Licenses, Friends Who Can Help,* and any other labels that cover your employability.

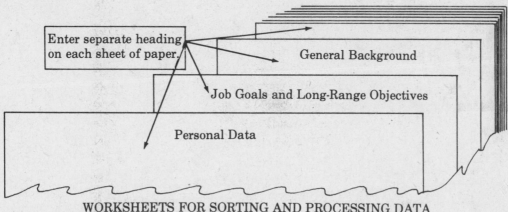

WORKSHEETS FOR SORTING AND PROCESSING DATA

With your draft sheets labeled, develop each sheet by the following four-step process:

- examine the draft-sheet heading—say, *Personal Data* or *Job Goals and Long-Range Objectives;*
- review notes and records for data that applies to that draft sheet;
- enter data appropriate to heading on draft sheet; for example, list all the jobs you have ever held on the *Work History* sheet; and
- check notes and records to insure inclusion of all pertinent data.

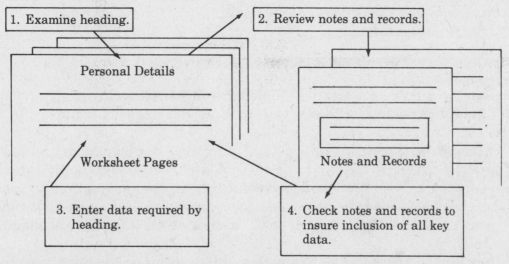

When you draft copy for one labeled sheet, move on to the next until you have transferred the key data from your personal records and self-analysis to the occupational worksheet you are drafting.

125

2. Placing the Occupational Worksheet in Final Form. Give your occupational worksheet draft a few days to cool, if you have the time. Return to it with a fresh outlook. Check it for accuracy and completeness. Make changes and additions and have it typed on 8½-by-11-inch sheets, since standard size is easiest to file and store.

The occupational worksheet you develop will serve you well when you draft your resume, providing the advantages depicted on the following diagram:

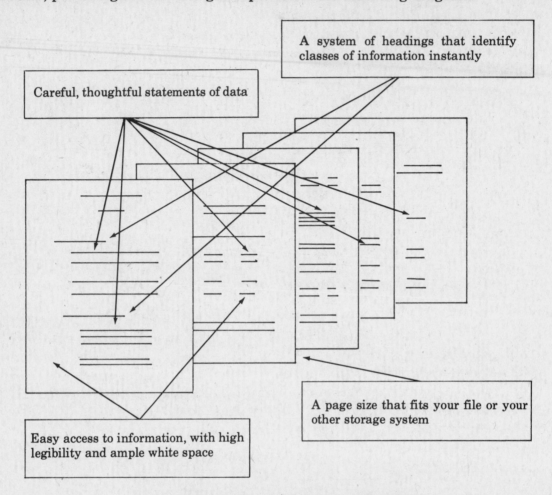

A system of headings that identify classes of information instantly

Careful, thoughtful statements of data

A page size that fits your file or your other storage system

Easy access to information, with high legibility and ample white space

TWO SECRETS OF THE CAREERIST

A careerist is a man or woman who plots his or her career carefully and thus achieves great success in life. Two important strategies are usually applied by the careerist.

1. The careerist takes great care in developing the best occupational worksheet possible very early in life and updates that worksheet constantly, whether looking for a job or not. Many persons keep their resumes on file and update these resumes when they need new jobs. Careerists prefer to keep the more basic, more private, more detailed document on file—the occupational worksheet.

2. The careerist always builds a career timetable into his occupational worksheet and tracks his progress according to that timetable. Note in the following timetable how the careerist can check where he should be at each point over the decade ahead and what preparation will bring him to the next point.

126

Project your chosen career ten years ahead, indicating target dates, positions you should hold on those dates, and the preparation you should have in progress at each target date.

CAREER TIMETABLE

Target Dates	Positions	Preparation Needed
1981	Become Bank Clerk	High school completed
1982	First Clerk	Take basic AIB courses
1983	Section Head	AIB courses and company training courses
1984	Section Head	Matriculate at university for BS in banking and finance
1985	Section Head	Continue evenings at university
1987	Platform Assistant	Continue university
1989	Assistant Manager	Complete university; take bank manager's course in company training program
1991	Assistant Manager	Take advanced banking courses; study banking independently
1992	Assistant Secretary	Continue study

SECTION 3
WRITING THE RESUME

THE FOUNDATION OF THE RESUME

An effective resume "sells" at a glance. It is built foursquare upon the right *job goals*, the right *data*, the right *design*, and the right *phrasing*.

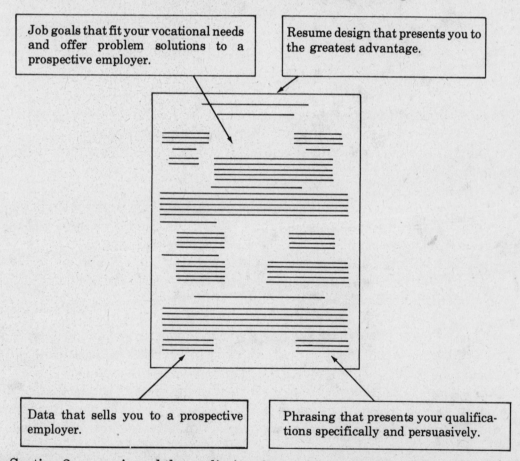

Job goals that fit your vocational needs and offer problem solutions to a prospective employer.

Resume design that presents you to the greatest advantage.

Data that sells you to a prospective employer.

Phrasing that presents your qualifications specifically and persuasively.

In Section 2, we reviewed the preliminaries to resume writing. We saw how the data needed in your resume is developed through the assembling of records, the analysis of self, and the surveying of the job market. This data is consolidated into an important tool called the occupational worksheet (pages 124, 179).

In the chapter you are now reading, you will see how the data summarized in the occupational worksheet is used to build your resume.

129

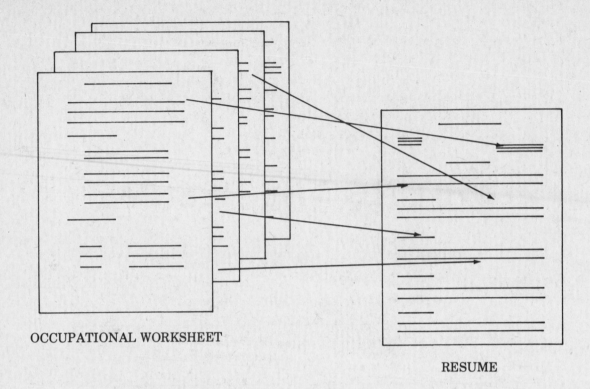

OCCUPATIONAL WORKSHEET

RESUME

The quality of paper and the patterning of data on the page whisper many things about you, often things you do not intend to say. The employer sees both a total design of black marks on white paper and a flashing of words, phrases, sentences, headings, data squares, and paragraphs.

- His sight drives at once to the center of vision (optical center) of the page. This center of vision always lies slightly above the actual center of the sheet (geometric center). From this center of vision, the reader measures unconsciously the balance of items above, below, to left, and right. He feels security within the margins. He senses order or disorder in the shape of surrounding lines and blocks of data.

- His sight tends to move up and down, *mostly down,* from that center of vision. Why? Because the 8½-by-11-inch sheet is taller than wide. In his uplift of vision, he seeks the big news of the resume. *Who is this applicant? What's he like? Where is he going? What can he do?* In his descent of vision, he follows paths formed by contours of data. He looks for the two main qualification units. *How well trained is this applicant? What experience has he had?*

- His sight focuses key words and phrases in that first up-and-down movement of eye. If key words materialize where he needs them, he judges the resume efficient, informative, and pleasing. He lifts his sight again and reads the resume carefully. If key words do not materialize or if he finds the way confusing, he becomes disturbed. His gaze falls off the page—*to someone else's resume.*

130

FOUR POINTS TO WATCH

When you compose your resume, you have four major concerns:

1. The Strategic Design for Total Resume Impact
2. The Strategic Grouping of Resume Data
3. The Strategic Selection of Resume Data
4. The Strategic Phrasing of Resume Data

Easy access to all your data in an occupational worksheet greatly simplifies the composing step. You do not have to take time out to develop data as needed.
Let us view these four major concerns one at a time.

STRATEGIC DESIGN FOR TOTAL RESUME IMPACT

The main guide to strategic resume design is common sense, fortified by a few very simple laws of design.

> ### TIP
> Use 8½-by-11-inch paper.

An 8½-by-11-inch sheet is preferred because it is standard for business and because it fits standard files. Resumes on odd-sized sheets are rejected as odd, difficult to handle, and impractical to file.

> ### TIP
> Use twenty-pound bond paper with cotton content, preferably white.

> ### TIP
> Prefer the one-page resume. If you must use a two-or three-page resume, develop also a one-page summary resume described on page 153 of this chapter.

One-page resumes are always preferred by prospects and personnel men, even for applicants with heavy experience. Younger applicants seldom have qualifications that justify more than a single sheet. Experienced applicants can always highlight their substantial experience on a single sheet and amplify that experience on a detailed resume. See pages 35 and 42.

Black-on-White Display

Pattern. The standard 8½-by-11-inch page provides 93½ square inches of white space for patterning the black-on-white display of resume data.

White space holds the total display on the page and helps the reader's eye get into data and find his way from point to point. Black space spells out resume information in words, phrases, sentences, and paragraphs. Vertical and horizontal lines are sometimes added to support the black-space patterning of words on the page.

Get the resume project under way with a sketch. The first impression your reader gets of your resume is the total design of black marks on white paper. Anticipate that total impression by blocking out the pattern of black lines the data of your resume will form.

- Concentrate on the concept of resume you think best for you.
- Anticipate the display units you will use to present such items as *Personal Data, Objective, Education, Experience,* and *References.*
- Arrange these units in a pattern that provides balance, rhythm, and emphasis.

The following exhibit shows a first sketch of a resume page and the thinking behind that sketch:

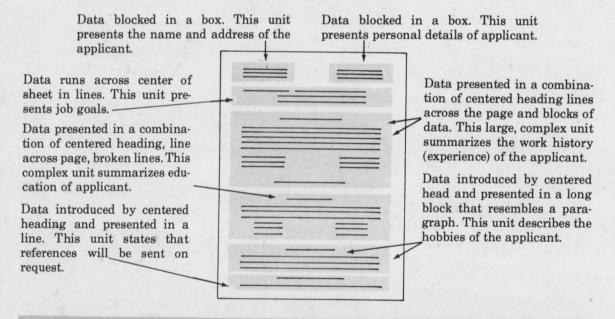

Data blocked in a box. This unit presents the name and address of the applicant.

Data blocked in a box. This unit presents personal details of applicant.

Data runs across center of sheet in lines. This unit presents job goals.

Data presented in a combination of centered heading, line across page, broken lines. This complex unit summarizes education of applicant.

Data introduced by centered heading and presented in a line. This unit states that references will be sent on request.

Data presented in a combination of centered heading lines across the page and blocks of data. This large, complex unit summarizes the work history (experience) of the applicant.

Data introduced by centered head and presented in a long block that resembles a paragraph. This unit describes the hobbies of the applicant.

As you sketch your early concept of resume, remember that your resume is primarily a display tool. The total shape of resume must harmonize all units of information in a single, clear, efficient, persuasive display.

Information is grouped on the resume in display units. Typical display units are headings, lines of words, and blocks of words. You have many different options for shaping each display unit.

Your address and telephone number, for example, is an important data group. You could display this data in a line of words across the page (see below). Such a line of words is a data display unit because it displays data attractively and persuasively.

----

189 Munn Avenue, Orange, N.Y., 19087; (212) 234-5678

Or you could display this data in a block of words on the left or right side of the page, or centered at the top of the page. This block of words is a data display unit (see below).

----

189 Munn Avenue
Orange, N.Y. 19087   OR HERE   OR HERE
(212) 234-5678

Whether you use a line or block depends on format chosen and the other display units appearing on that page. Data display units must harmonize within the total design of page. Note how a left-blocked address harmonizes with name, specialization, and personal data in a combination of lines and blocks (see below).

LINES ————————→ GLORIA M. BENTON
                 ↳ Systems Analyst

189 Munn Avenue   27 years old
Orange, N.Y. 19087 ←——————————————→ 5'7"; 132 pounds
(212) 234-5678   BLOCKS   Excellent health

TIP
Command a wide range of data display units.

Your ability to sketch an overall resume pattern is enhanced by the range of data display units you command. A *data display unit* is an information package you place upon the resume page—a heading, a line of data, a data box, or a paragraph. When you expand your knowledge of the kinds of data packaging available, you expand your ability to package each unit of data in a form that is most appropriate and that harmonizes within the total page display.

Basic Data Display Units

Here are some basic display units that every resume writer should know.

Headings. A heading is a word, phrase, or sentence that labels resume data. It may introduce the whole resume or it may appear within the resume as a *centered heading, side heading, cut-in heading,* or *data label.*

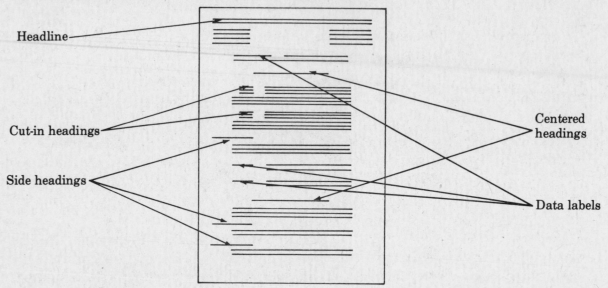

Opening the Resume

The problem of introducing the whole resume is governed by three important rules:

RULE 1. Open the resume with a display that captures favorable attention instantly, identifies you, and leads into resume.

RULE 2. Avoid the label *Resume* at the head of your presentation; it is redundant and corny.

RULE 3. Avoid the personal photograph unless you have powerful reason for using it; photographs are no longer standard for resumes since they encourage unfair labor practices and they often cause instant rejection.

What options are available for the opening of a resume?

One option is the *headline,* modeled upon the newspaper headline. It captures attention and spells out the big news. Headlines may consist of one or more lines and may be written in all capital letters or in a combination of capitals and lower case letters.

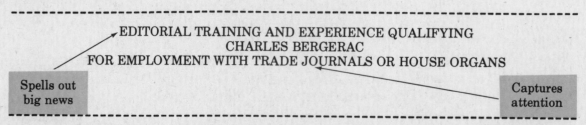

Another option is the job title opening, with statement of work performed placed before, after, or alongside your name.

THOMAS R. LARSEN

Training Supervisor and Employee Development Specialist

JAMES T. ATHENAKIS

20 Wilbur Way
Parsons, Vermont 09876
(123) 456 7890

ARCHITECT

Born: May 1, 1938
Marital Status: Married, six sons
Height: Six foot
Weight: 190 pounds
Health: Excellent

Still another option is opening with name and address and no special notice that the document is a resume. The appearance of the document will declare it a resume.

However, a resume for a professional man or woman—say, a doctor, dentist, or teacher—may be labeled *Vita* or *Curriculum Vitae*. See resumes on pages 39, 53, and 66.

Centered Headings

One of the most useful, but sadly neglected, data units of the resume is the centered heading. The centered heading has two great values:

- it delays and controls the downward plummet of eye on the page and flashes key data; and
- it helps balance the black-on-white design of the resume.

TIP

Consider centered headings as well as side headings when you develop your resume. If you feel that centered headings contribute, use them.

Note how the centered heading organizes display units efficiently in the following resume design.

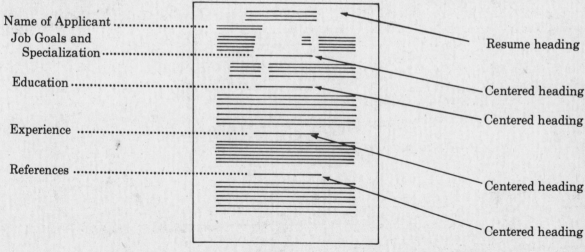

The centered heading works very well with the side heading. Each centered heading identifies a main resume section—say, *Education*. Each side heading identifies a subsection within that main section—say, *Ohio University*.

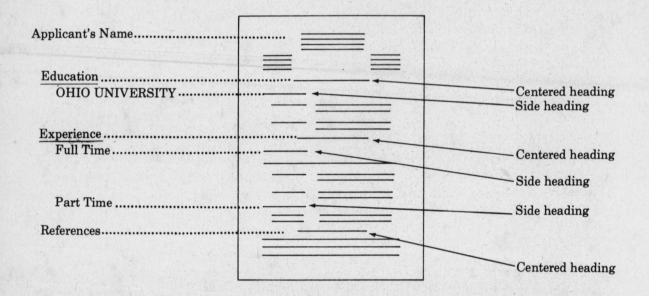

Centered headings may be written in all capital letters or in upper and lower case letters. These headings may or may not be underlined.

Sometimes two different ranks of centered heading may be used—capitalized centered headings for main division of resume data, and upper and lower case centered headings for secondary divisions. Side headings can indicate tertiary divisions.

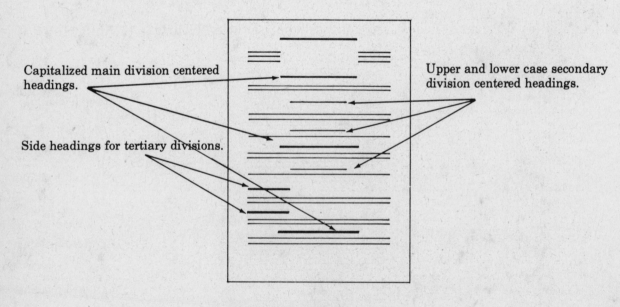

Centered headings may be reinforced with horizontal lines, either solid or broken.

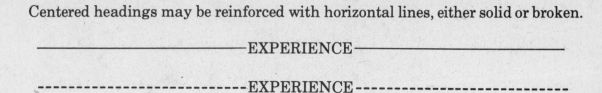

————————————————EXPERIENCE————————————————

- -EXPERIENCE- -

Study resumes on pages 12, 27, and 40 to see how these structural support lines add novelty, divide resume substance, and guide the downward sweep of eye to the right and left.

Side Headings

The side heading was the only divider used in the old-fashioned resume. Some resume writers think that it is the only heading permitted. As a result they often develop badly off-balance resumes with too much white space down the right hand side of the page. The side-headed resume does continue as the preferred divider for very simple resumes.

> **TIP**
>
> Use the side-headed resume for very simple resumes, but array material to avoid the badly off-balance appearance of most side-headed resumes.

See resumes on pages 15, 18, 20, and 28 for examples of side-headed resumes with carefully balanced data.

Simple Resume Divided with Side Headings

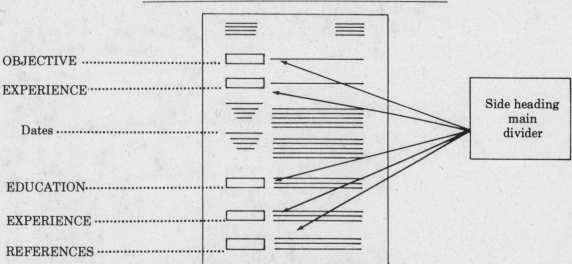

When side headings are used as main section dividers, they may be written in all caps or in upper and lower case letters. When side headings are used as subsection dividers within main sections, they are usually written in upper and lower case letters, underlined. An all-cap side heading may or may not be underlined. An upper and lower case side heading is always underlined. Side headings may appear on the same line with the data introduced or may appear on a line two spaces above that data.

EXPERIENCE: WELLINGTON ARMS HOTEL, Columbus, Ohio.

June 1976   Waitress in Gold Room, main dining room, and banquet
to Present   department.

DOLPHIN HOTEL, Clearwater, Florida

August 1974   Waitress in grill and relief cashier.
to June 1976

Side heading on same line as the data introduced.
(Also example of all-cap side heading, without underlining)

Experience:

Wellington Arms Hotel, Columbus, Ohio.

June 1976   Waitress in Gold Room, main dining room,
to Present   and banquet department.

Dolphin Hotel, Clearwater, Florida

August 1974   Waitress in grill and relief cashier.
to June 1976

Side heading placed two spaces above the data introduced.
(Also example of upper and lower case side heading with obligatory underlining)

An interesting combination of the centered and side heading is possible in the off-center heading with horizontal lines, either solid or broken.

——— EXPERIENCE ——

----- EXPERIENCE--

See resumes on page 81 and 85 for examples of this off-center heading.

Cut-In Headings

The cut-in heading both labels paragraphed data and provides access to data. The cut-in heading is placed at the center of a white-space box at the beginning of a paragraph or other long data block.

COMMERCIAL BANK OFFICER 1970-1973	Bresnafry National Bank, Ames, N.Y. Under the titles of Assistant Cashier and Assistant Vice-President, I managed a $50,000,000 commercial loan portfolio, with lending authority up to $100,000. This position placed me in direct charge of all credit analysis and the work of fifteen credit analysts. In addition, I coordinated the calls of all other

officers in the commercial lending phase of bank operations.

See resumes on pages 19 and 36 and note the value of cut-ins for applicants who must describe heavy experience in paragraphs.

Data Labels

The Data label serves as a tag to identify small units of resume data.

In the following illustration the data labels *Related Courses* and *Background Courses* tag two small units of resume data. Compare the operation of these data labels with that of the *centered heading* and the *side heading*.

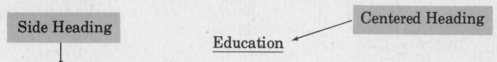

Side Heading   Education   Centered Heading

Dirksen University, Dirksen, N.Y.
Bachelor of Science, Mathematics, June 1980, in curriculum that included:

Computer-Related Courses	Background Courses
Advanced computer science	Finite mathematics I & II
COBOL programming	Mathematical analysis
FORTRAN programming	Statistical analysis I & II
Systems design and analysis	Functions of compiled variables
Quantitative communication	Advanced systems management
Digital computer techniques	Technical report writing

Data Labels

The versatility of the data label is illustrated in the following two exhibits. In both of these exhibits the data labels lie to the left of the unit labeled. In the first exhibit, the data labels are capitalized. In the second exhibit the data labels implement a secondary centered heading.

OBJECTIVE: To serve as managing publisher, editor-in-chief, or managing editor of trade journal or house organ.

SPECIALIZATION: Trade Journal and House Organ Editor

Data Display
Labels

139

Main centered heading in capital letters	→ EXPERIENCE

One year's experience as biochemistry aide at Georgeville University, Georgeville, Ga., June 1979 to present.

Secondary centered heading in upper and lower case	→Duties

Organizing experiments   Full charge of scheduling and planning experiments; setting up and dismantling of equipment; and coordinating research with other laboratory activities.

Dissecting specimens   Responsibility for all routine dissections and for conduct of toxicity tests.

Maintaining manual   Full charge of laboratory manual, including manual custody and accuracy of all entries made by staff.

Display labels for long blocks of data within larger display.

Lines of Data. A line of data is a long phrase or sentence that crosses a whole page or part of a page. Lines of data afford variety and help balance the resume page.

Note in the following exhibit how the line of data provides both variety and balance to the opening of a resume.

Line of Data

Thomas Rivington
Computer Programmer
395 Park Avenue, Buffalo, New York, 97503 Telephone (345) 598-7743

Personal

Born: February 7, 1953   Health: Excellent
Place of Birth: Ames, N.Y.   Height: 6'1"
Marital Status: Single   Weight: 170 pounds

Sometimes a line of data is spearheaded by a data display label.

JOB OBJECTIVE: Manager of hotel dining room or restaurant.

Sometimes several lines of data appear in a listing.

Military Skills
>   Trained and experienced in basic and advanced surveying.
>   Trained in standard earth-moving machinery.
>   Trained in elementary masonry and carpentry.

Blocked Data. Two or more successive lines of data form a data block. Data blocks may be square, long or uneven. A very familiar long data block, of course, is a paragraph.

Data blocks have two main values. They permit compact summaries of factual data like addresses, personal data, representative courses, and job duties. They provide mass for balancing and for contrasting with lines.

Square Data Blocks

Square blocks of data provide useful balancing shapes, as well as compact summaries. Note in the following illustrations how both courses and work experience details can be summarized in square blocks with one block balancing another.

SUMMARIZING COURSES IN SQUARE DATA BLOCKS

Computer-Related Courses	Background Courses
Advanced computer science	Finite mathematics I & II
COBOL programming	Mathematical analysis
FORTRAN programming	Statistical analysis I & II
Systems design and analysis	Functions of compiled variables
Quantitative communication	Advanced systems management
Digital computer techniques	Technical report writing

SUMMARIZING JOB DUTIES IN SQUARE DATA BLOCKS

Credit Manager, 1973-1980	Credit Manager, 1966-1973
Ames Drug Company, Ames, New York. Full charge of credit and collections; established policy; passed on all risks; and directed all collections. Losses less than one percent; sales increased by twenty-five per cent.	Post House Hotel, Ames, New York. Directed all extensions of credit in Guest and Banquet Departments. Established system for processing requests for credit. Served also as assistant controller of this 200-room hotel. Losses less than 1/2 of one percent.

Sometimes the square block is useful for balancing lines and white space.

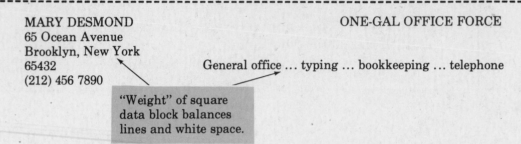

MARY DESMOND   ONE-GAL OFFICE FORCE
65 Ocean Avenue
Brooklyn, New York
65432   General office ... typing ... bookkeeping ... telephone
(212) 456 7890

"Weight" of square
data block balances
lines and white space.

Long Data Blocks (Paragraphs)

Long data blocks have two values on the resume page. They permit discussion through long phrases and full sentences and they provide another contrasting geometric shape. These long data blocks are usually called paragraphs, but they differ from the paragraphs of the standard page in two ways.

1. Resume paragraphs seldom open with indented lines. The best display effect is achieved if the paragraph is blocked or hung. Note how the poor display of the indented paragraph openings is improved with blocked and hung indention. See page 145 for further discussion of hung indention.

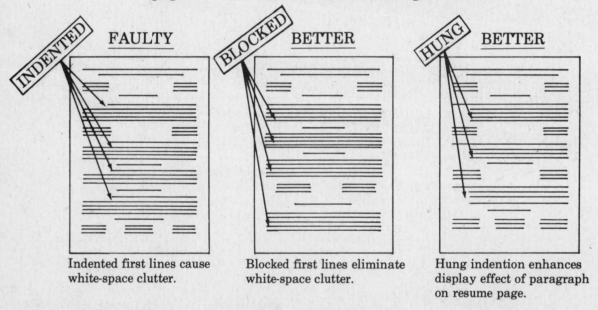

Indented first lines cause white-space clutter.

Blocked first lines eliminate white-space clutter.

Hung indention enhances display effect of paragraph on resume page.

As we noted on page 138, resume paragraphs can be labeled attractively with cut-in headings.

TIP

Make paragraphed data accessible to the eye with hung indention or cut-in headings when you develop semi-essay resumes; avoid the conventional indented paragraph, as a general rule. (See page 152 for discussion of Semi-essay resumes.)

2. Resume paragraphs consist of both full sentences and sentence fragments. Note how words and phrases are punctuated as though they were full sentences in the following example of a resume paragraph:

Biochemistry Research Aide

Georgeville University, Georgeville, Georgia.
1978-1980

Full Sentence

Dr. Thomas Twain, Director of the Georgeville Research Laboratory, gave me full responsibility for managing the laboratory. Responsible for all work schedules, for all purchases of supplies, and for all bookkeeping. In addition, conducted routine work of laboratory aide. Planned and scheduled experiments; dissected laboratory specimens; conducted toxicity tests; and maintained laboratory manuals.

Sentence Fragments

TIP

Take grammatical shortcuts when you phrase the resume, but avoid abbreviations and incompleteness of meaning. (See full discussion of phrasing on pages 162-166.)

Uneven Data Blocks

Some data groups consist of lines that are too uneven for square boxing. With a little juggling, these can usually be worked into some other geometric shape like a diamond or a pyramid.

Age:	25
Health:	Excellent
Height and Weight:	5'6", 130 pounds
Marital Status:	Single, no dependents

TIP

Avoid shapeless data blocks when you group resume data: seek the symmetrical shape that harmonizes with other shapes on the page.

White Space

TIP

Keep white space constantly in mind when you build a resume; the black space of data gains its display value from the white space of page.

Note how poor black-on-white design makes the following resumes inefficient and unattractive. In the resume to the left, black marks of data crowd all white space from the page. In the resume to the right, white space intrudes awkwardly among the data display units giving the resume a cluttered appearance.

FAULTY   FAULTY

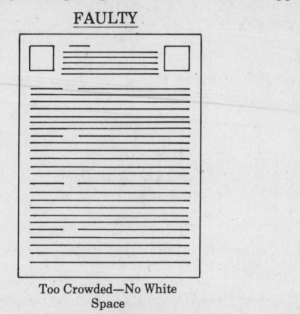

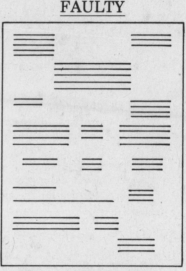

Too Crowded—No White   Cluttered—Eye Movement
Space   Confused

Conciseness of expression helps preserve the precious white space of the resume page. You can often trim data display units by rephrasing and discarding parts. Note for example how the data display unit to the left below can be justified if the long box of data is necessary to fill out the page. But white space can also be preserved, if needed, by deleting such labels as *Date of Birth* and *Height and Weight*.

Original   Trimmed

Date of Birth: June 1, 1945   Born June 1, 1945
Height and Weight: 5'11", 185 pounds   5'11", 185 pounds
Health: Excellent   Excellent health
Marital Status: Married, no children   Married, no children

White space can be used adroitly to help the eye get at key data.

One valuable technique for highlighting data is hung indention. Consider for example how the two job title entries in the display below are blocked. Note how each line begins flush with the left-hand margin.

EXPERIENCE

Editor-in-Chief, Textile Plastic Review, 245 Randall Street, Philadelphia, August, 1972 to Present.

Managing Editor, Beehive, Sterling Insurance Company, 16 State Street, Philadelphia, July, 1969 to August, 1972.

BLOCKED

144

Reading becomes easier and more exciting when the second line of each entry is indented.

EXPERIENCE

Editor-in-Chief, Textile Plastic Review, 245 Randall Street, Philadelphia,
 August, 1972 to Present.

Managing Editor, Beehive, Sterling Insurance Company, 16 State Street,
 Philadelphia, July, 1969 to August, 1972.

HUNG INDENTION

On page 142 you saw how hung indention is much more appropriate to resume display than the more usual paragraph indention.

Another technique for highlighting data with white space is the cut-in heading discussed on page 138.

Sometimes the problem is excessive white space. This excess occurs most commonly in:

- the side-headed resume (discussed on page 137);

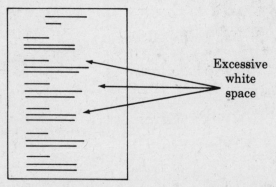

Excessive white space

- the two-or three-page resume in which data is distributed evenly over the first page, but ends near the top of the last page.

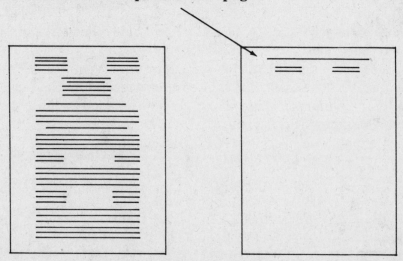

The best way to correct this fault in the long resume is to trim details to get all the data on a single sheet. If this reduction is impossible, expand details to distribute data evenly on the two or more pages.

Like any other tool, the design of a resume should be structural rather than ornamental. This structural design is formed mainly by the arrayal of words on the page. Occasionally, resumes benefit from a straight line or two that fill out the black pattern, guide the movement of the reader's eye, or divide elements.

Note for example how a single vertical line improves the structural efficiency of the resume illustrated below. This vertical line forms a path for the eye that integrates the scattered parts. It fills excessive white space. As it integrates, it also divides and emphasizes the parts that make up the whole.

AFTER LINE ADDED   BEFORE LINE ADDED

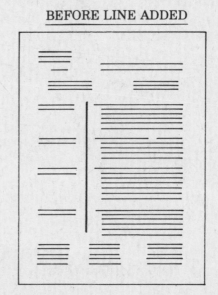

See the resumes on pages 12, 15, 16, 17, and 71 and note other ways that lines can be used to reinforce the structure of the resume.

Creative resumes—see pages 17 and 93—are a law unto themselves. These may use any kinds of decoration the resume reader can understand and accept.

Whatever kind of resume you write, avoid the corny—such as these garlands from the flowerbed of the typewriter keyboard.

****

John Jones
44 Spruce Street
Bloomfield, New Jersey 07003
(123) 456 7890

****

Balancing the Resume on the Page

TIP

Guide constantly on the *optical center* and the *center of balance* when you build the black-on-white display of resume page.

Your reader always focuses the page from its optical center. The optical center exists whether your page is blank or crowded with data. This center of vision relates to the physical center of balance for the sheet, if that sheet were suspended in space. You can locate the optical center of the 8½-by-11-inch sheet by measuring to a point one inch above the actual, or geometric, center of the page.

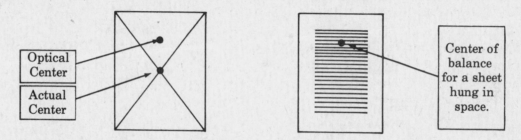

The importance of the optical center is illustrated in the following diagram. Knowing that the reader will focus the optical center first, the resume writer arranged his resume elements to make the most of that natural resting point of vision.

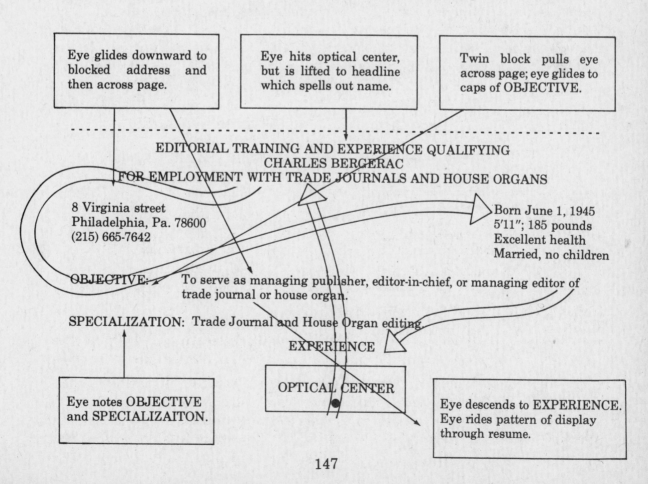

147

Locating the optical center makes possible strategic control of the reader's eye movements, but equally important it provides a base for shaping the black mass of data upon the page.

Without realizing it consciously, your reader *feels* physical balance as he holds your resume in his hands. The mass of data you place on the page has *weight* in your reader's feelings and thoughts. This weight creates a new center of balance—which artists call an *occult (or psychic) center of balance.*

When you add a pattern of black data to the white space of resume page, be careful not to upset the stability of the page. Note how the design center of data shape clashes with the optical center, throwing each of the resumes designed below off balance.

FAULTY

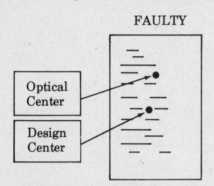

FAULTY

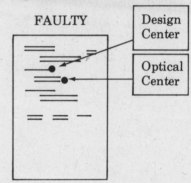

The occult (or psychic) center of balance seldom coincides absolutely with the physical center of balance (center of vision). Nor is this balance desirable. Such absolute balance would prove deadly dull to the reader's eye. However, the balance of page must be appropriate for an 8½-by-11-inch sheet held in front of a reader.

Note how the absolute balance of the resume diagrammed in the model to the left below is static and uninteresting. Note how the difference between physical balance and occult balance makes the resume to the right come alive. Yet note that both do balance in a way that maintains equilibrium for the 8½-by-11-inch sheet.

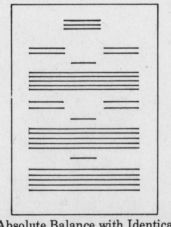

Absolute Balance with Identical
Physical and Occult Balance
Points

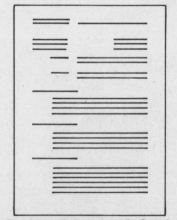

Exciting Balance with Occult
Balance Point to Left of
Physical Balance Point

The so-called off-balance or off-center resume design attained by placing the design center slightly to the right of the optical center is not really off center or off balance. It is simply balanced on an occult center, a balance needed because resumes are usually heavy with left-hand side headings.

The 8½-by-11-inch sheet is taller than wide. When a sheet is taller than wide, the reader's eye tends to move up and down, mostly down. A widest bottom margin counters this natural downward plunge of vision. A second-widest top margin counters any upward thrust. Narrower side margins invite lateral movement. The right margin is usually the narrowest on the sheet. The actual size of margins can vary, but these ratios must be maintained. In no event should the bottom margin be less than *one inch* and the left side margin less than *half an inch*.

Note how the margins in the following resumes are correct in ratio even though they vary in inches.

CORRECT MARGIN RATIO   CORRECT MARGIN RATIO

Note how the margins in the following resumes are faulty in ratio.

FAULTY MARGIN RATIO   FAULTY MARGIN RATIO

149

Your first sketch of resume layout gets the resume project underway. The realities of grouping, selecting, and phrasing actual data generally call for revisions of your basic plan. Your name and address which you planned to center at the top of the sheet may look better in the upper left-hand corner of the sheet. The system of side headings may not prove adequate for dividing your material. You may find centered main headings more advantageous, with side headings used to subdivide main data groups.

This process of shaping the total pattern of black on white continues until the final typing of the resume. Even then, revise if necessary. As you view the typed resume, you may feel that the page is monotonous and static with too many units in square blocks. Some of these units may be more attractive in lines across the page. You may feel that the shapes of some display units clash with the shapes of others, that the eye gets trapped somewhere or flies off into space. You may feel that the resume is packed too tight or too loose.

Revise and retype, if necessary. The right resume can open doors that will affect you for the rest of your life.

THE STRATEGIC GROUPING OF RESUME DATA

As we noted on page 132, you must think of data groups as you conceive and sketch your basic resume design.

The data groups you choose for your resume are dictated in part by the objective of your resume and in part by qualifications you possess as an employable person. For example, every resume must include your *name, address, personal details, objective, education,* and—if you have ever worked—your *work history.* As an employable person, you may find it necessary also to include data on *licenses held, languages or publications.*

The order of data on the resume page is dictated in part by the expectations of the reader and in part by your tactical needs. For example, your reader expects your name, address, and telephone number at the top of the sheet. You have no choice but to place this essential information at the beginning of your resume. But you do have options in placing your *education* and *work history.* If *education* is your strong qualification, place it first and develop it fully. If *work history* is your strong qualification, place it first and develop it fully.

A *format* is the arrangement or makeup of a document. The two resumes that follow differ in format. The resume to the left is highly tabulated; it resembles a data table with its system of headings and brief data entries. The resume to the right is also tabulated, but much less than the resume to the left. The resume to the right has fewer headings and much longer data entries; it has many characteristics of a paragraphed page. These two resumes illustrate two different formats—the *fully tabulated* and the *semi-essay*.

Fully Tabulated Resume   Semi-Essay Resume

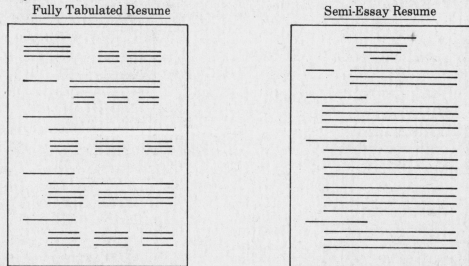

Resumes appear in seven different formats—*fully tabulated, semi-essay, brochure, synopsis (abridged), chronological,* and *functional*. These classes of format, however, overlap. A fully tabulated resume could be chronological or functional; a functional resume could have chronological features. We shall see how in a moment. The main point to remember is that you must choose a format with general makeup features that serve you best and you must adapt the features of that format to your advantage.

Let us review the main characteristics of each resume format and the advantages of each.

The Fully Tabulated Resume. All resumes use devices of the data table, but some as we have just seen, are more highly tabulated than others. Note the resumes on pages 20, 22, and 30 for illustrations of fully tabulated resumes.

The fully tabulated resume permits easy reading, a roundup of many kinds of data, and a spatial relating of one kind of data with another. It does not permit discussion, analysis, and interpretation.

This format is often recommended for younger, less experienced applicants with varied qualifications like school courses, extracurricular activities, hobbies, and occasional jobs. Less experienced applicants must display a variety of data because they have little depth of experience demanding analysis and explanation.

TIP

Prefer the fully tabulated resume if you are young and less experienced, with varied qualifications like school courses, extracurricular activities, hobbies, and occasional jobs.

The Semi-Essay Resume. This format, as we have seen, uses fewer devices of the data table and a number of long data entries.

Note, however, that the amount of tabulation and the length of entries can be varied to suit your advantage. You may use the moderate semi-essay resume format depicted to the left below, the extreme semi-essay resume format depicted to the right, or any in-between variation that serves you best.

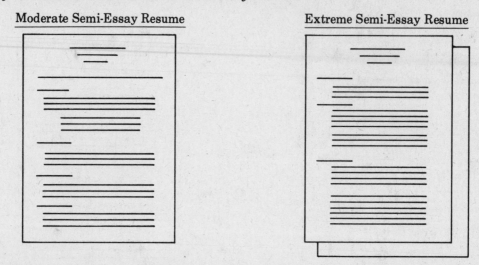

Moderate Semi-Essay Resume · Extreme Semi-Essay Resume

(See moderate semi-essay resumes on pages 19, 33, and 41. See extreme semi-essay resumes on pages 36, 43, and 53.)

You may also develop a resume that combines high tabulations and semi-essay elements:

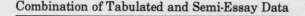

Combination of Tabulated and Semi-Essay Data

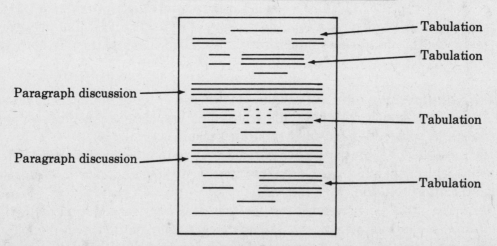

Tabulation
Tabulation
Paragraph discussion
Tabulation
Paragraph discussion
Tabulation

TIP

Introduce semi-essay elements to the extent needed to develop heavy qualifications.

The amount of discussion (essay) material you introduce in your resume varies with your experience. The older and more experienced applicant may find the more

152

extreme semi-essay resume advantageous. Discussion material occupies more space than highly tabulated data. Too much discussion may defeat the purpose of the resume.

The Brochure Resume. A brochure resume is a multipage, semi-essay resume in a leaflet format. It is reproduced on 11-by-17-inch sheets which are folded into 8½-by-11-inch pages. It may consist of four, eight, or even twelve pages.

The brochure resume has two main advantages:

1. It provides a convenient vehicle for presenting two or more pages of data.
2. It accommodates a separately typed, specially designed application letter on the brochure cover.

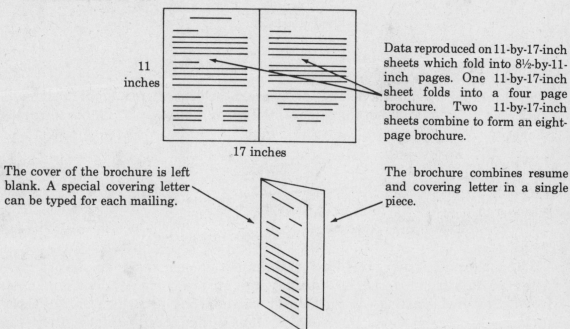

11 inches

17 inches

Data reproduced on 11-by-17-inch sheets which fold into 8½-by-11-inch pages. One 11-by-17-inch sheet folds into a four page brochure. Two 11-by-17-inch sheets combine to form an eight-page brochure.

The cover of the brochure is left blank. A special covering letter can be typed for each mailing.

The brochure combines resume and covering letter in a single piece.

The brochure is always conspicuous, which may be an advantage or a disadvantage.

But the brochure resume has some very significant disadvantages. It requires great skill to develop. Professional resume writers like this format because it impresses the applicant and helps justify the fee charged. It is long-drawn-out and clashes with the basic concept implied in the word *resume*.

> **TIP**
>
> Consider grand-manner resumes, like the brochure resume, if—and only if—you have good reason.

The Synopsis (Abridged) Resume. The synopsis resume is a summary of a summary. It is very brief and it implies the existence of a longer, fuller resume. Examples of synopsis resumes appear on pages 32, 35, 42, 62, 90, and 102. Note that each synopsis resume abridges data from a longer resume that immediately follows.

A synopsis resume is always written after the longer resume has been composed. An applicant with heavy qualifications writes a full resume—say, two or three pages—summarizing his qualifications. He then abstracts from this full resume a short resume highlighting his qualifications. This *synopsis* or *abridged resume* becomes his basic working or general contact resume. He holds his longer resume in reserve, submitting it only when a detailed resume is requested. The following exhibit illustrates a synopsis (abridged) resume:

The data for a synopsis resume, of course, is selected from a longer resume. This data may be summarized in one or more brief paragraphs or in a number of single-line displays.

TIP

Develop a synopsis resume as a general contact resume if you have heavy qualifications.

The Chronological (Time Order) Resume. Some resumes emphasize time by arraying data in time order and displaying dates prominently. The time order is usually inverted, starting with the latest item and working backwards. The resumes on pages 12, 17, and 23 are chronological, that is time order, resumes.

Under *Work History*, a chronological resume starts with the latest job held; then it displays the second-latest job; and then the third-latest job. Under *Education* the chronological resume starts with the latest educational experience, then the second-latest, and then earlier experiences if pertinent.

A chronological resume may be a fully tabulated resume, a semi-essay resume, or a creative resume.

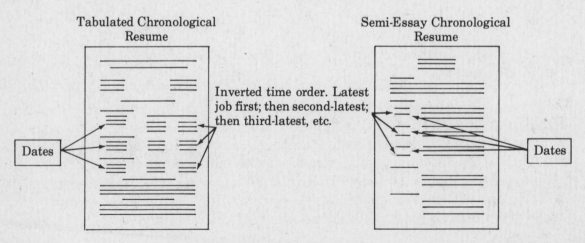

Tabulated Chronological Resume

Semi-Essay Chronological Resume

Inverted time order. Latest job first; then second-latest; then third-latest, etc.

Dates

Dates

The chronological resume has one great advantage—prospective employers like it. An applicant is easy to judge when his worth is cast in inverted time order. But this order is not always advantageous for the applicant, especially when his latest job is not his most impressive.

The Functional Resume. Some resumes emphasize kinds of work (functions) without maintaining any particular time order. Study the resumes on page 93 and 94 and observe how function is stressed and little emphasis is given to time. Note how the synopsis resumes on pages 32, 35, and 62 are also functional resumes.

The main advantage of the functional resume is the prominence it gives to actual achievement. Consider a systems designer who wants to stress the depth of his experience in systems design. Reviewing his work experience and his training, he groups everything that qualifies him for a job in system design as a first qualification entry in his resume.

Within this entry, the applicant cites the work he has performed in systems design and any training he has had for this work. The first item may or may not be his latest job, but it is a job that relates to systems design. He may include in this section jobs and training scattered in time. The main disadvantage of the functional resume is that prospective employers have to work out their own chronologies. Note in the following work history how it is possible to omit dates entirely in a functional resume, but this practice is not recommended:

EXPERIENCE AS OPERATIONAL AUDITOR

Fifteen years of heavy operational auditing experience with major chemical products manufacturer and large power and gas public utility, after thorough training in engineering (BS in chemical engineering) and accounting (MBA in accounting).

AUDIT MANAGER — Nine years' experience with Thales Chemical, Inc., as Operational Auditor (four years) and Audit Manager (five years). I designed the basic systems and procedures for enlarging the financial audit of this company to a full audit that included engineering design, production, and control.

My system integrated perfectly with the financial audit and qualified me for the top auditing post when the incumbent Audit Manager retired.

I was responsible for both the financial and production audit of this company and reported directly to the President. In this work I managed a staff of sixty.

INTERNAL AUDITOR — Six years' experience with Metropolitan Utility as Internal Auditor. I had full charge of auditing the reviews conducted by contract analysts, including audits of field performance in vegetation, gas, and wiring and audits of contracts and disbursements.

When you select for the functional resume, keep function foremost in mind. You can, of course, insert dates within the body of presentation. For example, the author of the above could have placed actual dates, rather than (four years) and (five years) in the entry for Audit Manager. Names of companies are sometimes omitted in functional resumes.

TIP

Use a chronological order of presentation if your career advancement has been progressive and the job you seek is the same as your latest job; use a functional order if strict time order places you at a disadvantage.

The Creative Resume. Applicants in the arts, advertising, promotion, and other creative areas sometimes prepare resumes that break with standard resume format. See the resumes on pages 17 and 93 for examples of creative resumes.

Creative resumes are advantageous when addressed to other creative persons. They identify the applicant as creative and provide an example of creative imagination which is desirable in the job sought. A dance teacher, for example, might get into stride with the owner of a dance school by preparing a resume in script type that looks like the invitation to a ball. A theatrical producer or dramatic coach might capture the interest of a prospective employer by shaping a resume that looks like a theatre program. His name could be presented under the heading *Cast;* his address under the heading *Setting;* his early life under the heading *Prelude;* and his education and experience under Act I, Act II, and Act III.

A creative resume must exercise imagination, but it must also supply the reader with the data he needs. Note how the creative resume for a mod clothing sales clerk on page 93 handles his ability to earn profits.

TIP

Use a creative resume for creative fields only; generally avoid the creative in banking, commerce, transportation, and industry.

Relate this observation to the tip on the brochure resume (page 153). Avoid extremes, unless you have good reason to do otherwise. Decorative touches, colored mountings, patches, pink ribbons, and other gimmicks may capture attention, and even impress, but they also hazard instant rejection with most prospective employers.

The resume format you select provides a general guide for choosing data classes and grouping data units strategically on the resume page. This strategy, of course, like all your other planning strategies, should be included in your latest sketch of resume design.

THE STRATEGIC SELECTION OF RESUME DATA

The particular data you select for your resume is governed in part by the format you choose, but it is also governed by the actual qualifications you possess. If you have prepared an occupational worksheet, the data you need is readily accessible but in too great an abundance for any single resume. The occupational worksheet summarizes *all* the data available on you as a careerist. A resume includes only that data which helps you achieve your resume objective.

Resume data is grouped in two main classes—a *basic data class* and an *optional data class*. Basic resume data must be included because your reader expects it; if you don't include it your reader will think something is wrong and reject you at once. Optional data may be included or omitted; the choice is yours.

Basic Resume Data. No matter what kind of resume you write, you must include your name, your address and telephone number, your personal details, your job objective, your educational history, and your work history.

TIP

Always indicate your name in full early in the resume. If your name is difficult to pronounce, provide a phonetic respelling. (See page 56.) You may place your name to the right, center, or left; you may work your name into a headline; but make it prominent.

TIP

Always indicate your address and telephone number early in the resume. Be certain to include zip number and area code. If you have a temporary address and a permanent address, indicate both.

Address and Phone to May 30	Address and Phone after May 30
456 Clark Street	2000 Michigan Boulevard
Ames, Iowa 09876	Cairo, Illinois 76543
(123) 456 7890	(321) 654 0987

TIP

Always present such personal data as age, height, health, and marital status, including number of dependents. If pertinent, include place of birth and financial condition. Personal data is placed preferably at the beginning of the resume because that is where personnel people like to see it. This data may also be placed at the end of the resume.

TIP

Always indicate or imply your job objective early in the resume. If pertinent, indicate or imply also your career objective and specialization.

The most emphatic way to indicate your job objective is to have a heading or data label *Objective* or *Job Objective* followed by your actual objective. (See resumes on pages 12, 13, 16, 17, and 18.) You imply your job objective when you state your specialization—say *Tool Maker* or *Veterinarian*—early in your resume. (See resumes on pages 23, 30, 36, and 49.) You also imply your objective when you use a headline. (See resumes on page 77, 90 and 98.) A synopsis, discussed fully on page 153, may be used to present your objective.

TIP

If you have no substantial experience, indicate your education before you indicate your work history. If you have a year or more of solid experience, indicate your work history first. (See resumes on pages 11 and 94 for education before work history. See resumes on pages 75 and 80 for work history before education.)

TIP

Specify your high school or trade school diploma if you have no higher level of education. If you have a college degree, specify your high school only if you feel it pertinent. If you have a graduate degree, specify both your graduate and your undergraduate degrees. Array your education in decreasing order of importance, starting with your highest attainment. (See resumes on pages 23 and 26 for high school and trade school educational histories. See resume on page 48 for arrayal of college degrees.)

TIP

Spell out your degrees, indicating dates, major, specialization, and colleges or universities. If your college minor supports your objective, mention that too. List representative courses, credits, and even grades if they support your objective. Prefer grade letters A, B, and C to numbers like 3.5 in indicating average. (See resume on page 87.)

TIP

If you attended school on scholarships or fellowships or if you earned any or all of your tuition, indicate these conditions in your resume. (See resumes on pages 17 and 18.)

TIP

Mention extracurricular activities (a) if education is your main qualification; (b) if they are unusual—president of student council, state typing champion; (c) if they give proof of your honesty, responsibility, or personality; and (d) if they support your job objective (See resumes on pages 69, 74, 88, and 108.)

TIP

Give fewer details about your earlier education as you advance in maturity and experience. If you have completed college, give few if any details about high school. If you have worked for five or more years, give fewer details about colleges—especially extracurricular activities.

TIP

Place your work history (experience) before your education if solid, fulltime experience extends for at least a year. Unless you employ a functional resume (See pages 63 through 65) indicate your work history in inverted time order, beginning with the latest job held and working backwards.

TIP

Disguise company names in whole or in part if you are changing jobs and do not want your present employer to know about your plans. Remember that if you fail to get the new job, your present employer will lose all confidence in you. The best way to disguise your work history is to send out a synopsis or qualification resume that does not identify employers. (See resumes on pages 32, 35, and 42.) Consider the third-party technique; that is, have some third party, say, a placement director send your resume out without disclosing your name.

TIP

Identify duties performed, responsibilities, number of persons managed, and achievements in your work history. If company is not well known, indicate product, number of employees, and capitalization. (See resumes on pages 36, 49, and 52.)

TIP

Indicate months for jobs held less than three years—January, 1979 to June, 1980. Label part-time jobs as *part time*. Check your resume for time gaps; your reader will. If you see a time gap anywhere, repair it. (See resumes on pages 46, 71, and 88.)

TIP

Support your assertions. If you state or imply possession of certain skills or personality traits, list jobs performed, offices held, or honors received to convince reader. (See resumes on pages 17, 22, 40, and 64.)

TIP

Whether you present references on your resume, or merely promise to send them, always display a reference heading.

Originally, references were an obligatory section of the resume. A valid resume always carried the names and addresses of responsible persons who could vouch for the character of the applicant and the truth of his statements. Usually, each major area of education and experience was backed up by a reference.

Today you may or may not include actual references, but you must make some provision for references on the resume page. If you include references, give name, title, address, and telephone number of each person you list. Make all references professional and pertinent to the resume that is, deans, principals, teachers, company officers who have directed your work. Avoid relatives and social references like uncles, neighbors, and family friends. Always notify references that you have given their names.

Giving references on the resume has advantages. It makes your resume ring solid with conviction.

But listing references has disadvantages that you must also consider.

- Your present employer may learn that you want to change jobs if you list any references. It's a small world and the word spreads.

- Your prospect may screen you out without an interview. Many prospects telephone references listed or send them questionnaires before offering interviews. Your objective is to get to the interview table.

- Your prospects may annoy your references with a pileup of pre-interview queries. It may be better to give references after the prospect shows genuine interest.

Note on pages 15, 17, 18, and 19 how reference sections are included, but how actual references are promised rather than listed.

Optional Resume Data. In addition to the basic resume data which all resumes must carry, you may include also such optional resume data classes like:

Background (See resume on page 39.)
Financial Condition (See resumes on pages 42 and 78.)
Hobbies (See resumes on pages 20 and 30.)
Honors and Awards (See resumes on pages 22 and 65.)
Languages (See resumes on pages 67 and 98.)
Licenses Held (See resumes on pages 60 and 78.)
Military Service (See resumes on pages 16 and 33.)
Patents Held (See resume on page 106.)
Professional Affiliations (See resumes on pages 65 and 104.)
Publications (See resume on page 58.)
Synopsis (See resumes on pages 77 and 81.)
Skills (See resumes on pages 34 and 28.)
Travel (See resumes on pages 92 and 98.)
Union Membership (See resume on page 60.)

TIP

Include any class of data that supports your objective, but avoid irrelevant data classes.

Not only may you include any or all of the optional data classes listed above, but you may even invent and include such data classes as *European Subways Studied,*

Sanskrit Translations, or *Knowledge of Ethnic Preferences.* If a class of data deserves emphasis, include it.

Do not include data classes like financial condition, hobbies, languages, or travel without good reason. A waitress might mention her hobby of tennis to show that she is agile or her knowledge of foreign languages if she seeks work in a cosmopolitan setting. But a full-charge bookkeeper would gain little from mentioning his hobby of gun collecting or his knowledge of five languages if these categories do not relate to his work.

> **TIP**
>
> Emphasize in a separate data category any data of special importance in the job you seek.

If you must hold certain licenses, professional affiliations, or union memberships to qualify for the job you seek, place them in special categories and identify them with a centered heading, side heading, or prominent data label. (See resumes on pages 78 and 104.) Always give details, including dates. If skills in machine operation or technical procedures are important, emphasize them separately, (See resumes on pages 12 and 34.) Military experience may be touched on lightly in your personal data, may be grouped with your education or work experience, or may be presented in its own category. But always stress military experience in its own category if it supports your job objective—say, in getting a job as a security manager, as a teacher in a military school, or as a member of a firm that deals with military clientele. (See resumes on pages 16 and 33.)

> **TIP**
>
> Use *Background* and *Synopsis* categories to summarize data of general importance.

Sometimes it is valuable for a prospective employer to know something of your early life or some period of your life that is not covered in your education or work history. This data is given in a *General Background* section like the following:

General Background

Born in Saranac Lake, N.Y., but moved with family to Mount Vernon, Ohio, at age of seven. Mother, father, and five brothers still reside in Mount Vernon. Raised in Mount Vernon, attending college at nearby Kenyon. Lived with family until coming to New York to enter advertising.

Sometimes it is valuable to summarize your job objective and your main qualifications early in your resume. This summary is called a synopsis. A synopsis provides an overview for a long complicated resume and permits comment on subjects like changing careers. Consider for example the production manager who decided to enter operational auditing. He introduced his resume with the following synopsis.

Operational Auditor. Production manager with fifteen years of heavy industrial and accounting experience, holding a bachelor's degree in accounting and a master's degree in industrial engineering, ready to assume major responsibility as an operational auditor with a large manufacturer.

THE STRATEGIC PHRASING OF RESUME DATA

Resume data must be phrased efficiently, informatively, and persuasively within the limitations of the resume page. Despite the variety of possible formats and approaches, some helpful rules exist to guide you in phrasing your resume.

TIP
Adapt your resume to your reader.

Your reader is always a potential employer. He is interested in what you can do for him. Choose phrases that reveal you as a solution to his problems. Avoid phrases that disclose your own selfish interests.

Selfish	Adapted
Objective: To gain work satisfaction and job security in a position as a management accountant and eventually enjoy the prestige of becoming an officer in a stable, understanding corporate atmosphere.	Objective: To contribute my management accounting insights to the reduction of costs and the increase of profits in an organization with challenging accounting problems, and thus earn my way to higher executive responsibility.

TIP
Consider *tone* constantly when you phrase your resume.

Tone is the emotional impact of your resume. Despite the myth of resume objectivity, all resumes convey some kind of emotional impact. If that emotional impact is appropriate, it will work to your advantage. If that emotional impact is inappropriate, it will undermine your resume.

All resumes should *seem* objective, even though true objectivity is impossible. The *myth of resume objectivity* assumes that a resume is a fact sheet. This myth must be preserved in all of its outward appearances. Highly colored modifiers, opinion words, and intensifiers should be excluded. Prefer concrete, specific nouns and verbs.

Opinion	Facts
my trustworthy nature	disbursed $75 million in funds annually for the past ten years
persistent leadership that constantly overcame obstacles	supervisor of 300 skilled technicians and laborers, deployed to repair 90 to 100 breakdowns weekly

Concrete, specific nouns and verbs provide a tone of motivation, alertness, confidence, modesty, and professional enthusiasm, without destroying objectivity. Avoid especially *resumese,* the cliché generalities that cheat your reader of the detail he wants. High on the list of resumese is "exercised great responsibility (mature judgment, constant vigilance, persistent leadership)," "provided valuable assistance," "was accorded full recognition," and "my trustworthy nature."

Generalities and Clichés	Specific, Concrete Language
Biochemistry Research Aide Georgeville University Georgeville, Georgia 1975-1978	Biochemistry Research Aide Georgeville University Georgeville, Georgia 1975-1978
Duties: Provided valuable assistance to research staff; performed important general laboratory duties; exercised great responsibility.	Duties: Planned and scheduled experiments; dissected laboratory specimens; conducted toxicity tests; and maintained laboratory manual.
My trustworthy nature was accorded full recognition on the part of the management.	Received three commendations from the executive committee—two for intelligent initiative, and one for follow-up responsibility.
Exercised mature leadership.	Selected and trained five assistant supervisors and saved the company $25,000 in staff recruiting fees.

Stating the facts in concrete, specific detail makes it possible for you to balance modesty and confidence without faintheartedness or boasting.

Sometimes a little interpretation of the facts is needed. Consider the bank officer who held the title *assistant manager* when he was actually a branch manager up for promotion to the post of *assistant vice-president.* He wrote the following entry on his resume, giving the data the interpretation it required:

Full charge of Prescott Branch, First National Bank of Bresnafry. Despite official title of Assistant Manager, was actually the branch manager. Title of Assistant Vice-President recommended and expected in April 19——.

If you precede details with an interpretive heading, you can subtly influence the value your reader places on those details.

One merit of a headline is its capacity to define tone. A senior engineer desirous of establishing a tone of dignified professional reserve used the following headline:

EDUCATION AND EXPERIENCE QUALIFICATIONS
OF JOHN R. BENNETT
AS DESIGNER OF ELECTRONIC INSTRUMENTS

Had he desired to enhance the persuasiveness of his resume he could have used the headline:

```
-----------------------------------------------------------------------------
         ELECTRONIC-DESIGN EDUCATION AND EXPERIENCE
         JOHN R. BENNETT CAN BRING TO YOUR COMPANY
-----------------------------------------------------------------------------
```

Both of these headlines are good. Which one is better depends on the occasion. Note how the following headline is creative, yet it has a stately dignity appropriate to the writer and her readers:

```
-----------------------------------------------------------------------------

                          An Invitation to the Dance
                                    with
                          Helen MacInness Cameron

-----------------------------------------------------------------------------
```

Centered and side headings can also be made more interpretive. Tradition has established resume heads like *Experience, Education,* and *References.* Very often it is advantageous to make these stereotypes more specific. Sometimes it is strategic to make these traditional headings more interpretive.

The data class *Objective* can be implied in a headline, as we have just seen, or in a synopsis, as discussed on page 161. The *Experience* heading could be replaced by *Executive and Professional Staff Positions.* The *Education* heading could be replaced by *Professional Training in Sophisticated Systems Design.*

When you label subunits like representative courses or extracurricular activities, consider the possibility of interpretive labels. The subunit label *Representative Courses* is traditional and quite acceptable. Yet a nurse with a bachelor's degree might consider *Key Academic and Clinical Courses* as a label for her representative courses. A young man seeking a job as a management trainee might label his extracurricular activities *Leadership in Student Activities.*

When you label subunits like positions held or job duties, consider the possibility of interpretive labels. You could use the traditional heading *Position Held* or *Job Duties;* you could use the official job title—*Administrative Assistant*—or your rank as an officer—*Assistant Vice-President;* or you could use a descriptive label that identifies the kind of work you did—*Supervisor of 300 Skilled Technicians and Laborers.*

How far you go in heightening the emotional impact of your resume depends on who you are, whom you address, and what kind of work you want. If you are older, if your prospective employer is older, or if you want to work in fields like accounting, banking or manufacturing, make your tone conservative. If you are younger, if your prospective employer is younger, or if you want to work in fields like advertising, the arts, entertainment, or sales, make your tone livelier. Today's trend is toward the lively, but old values are strongly entrenched.

TIP

Stress the positive and constructive; minimize or omit negative.

You can improve the emotional appeal of your resume by advancing the positive and de-emphasizing or omitting the negative. Your resume is a view of employable you. No one is perfect and you are under no obligation to detail your imperfections. Note how the resumes exhibited in this book constantly advance the positive.

Guard against the negative statement of ideas that are basically positive. Instead of saying "performed transactions not going beyond the general ledger," say "performed transactions through the general ledger." Instead of saying "as an officer of the firm never left for home until well after midnight," say "as an officer worked until well after midnight every workday."

Guard against the unnecessary introductions of a negative. If you have a strong work history, but lack a high school diploma, why bring up the category of *Education* at all. If you have never worked, omit the category *Experience* entirely. Don't write *Experience: None.*

If the negative is unavoidable, you may have to explain it. For example, the bank officer with the title *assistant manager* explained how the title was misleading.

The negative is a special problem in the resume because resumes are always screened with a *negative bias*. Resume readers simplify their lives by scanning first for *knockouts*—resume items that justify rejection. Words like *no, not* and *lack* catch their eyes immediately and invite instant rejection.

TIP
Phrase concisely.

The key to concise resume phrasing is preference for the specific, concrete noun and the strong verb. Resume format permits many language shortcuts—one-word entries, short phrases, sentence fragments, and data tabulation. Always think first of the specific concrete noun or the strong verb when you enter data on the resume page. Specific nouns and concrete verbs spare you modifiers and connectives.

Strong verbs are especially valuable because they reduce the number of words needed to convey a dynamic idea. When you present items of education or work history, use verbs without subjects. Instead of "I earned a promotion within three months," say "earned promotion within three months" or "promoted within three months."

Using verbs without subjects spares you the overuse of the pronoun "I." Many persons imagine that "I" is offensive in itself and they awkwardly substitute "the writer" or even more awkwardly shift to the third person "he" or "she." If you must use "I," then use it. Never refer to yourself as "he" or "she" in a resume. But take advantage of the language shortcuts permitted in the resume and use verbs without subjects when you can.

Prefer verbs that are strong in action to verbs that imply receiving or accepting. Prefer active voice to passive voice. Prefer doing verbs to being verbs.

Weak	Action Verbs
given instructions in computer programming	mastered computer programming
received instructions in . . .	studied . . ., learned . . .
was promoted to . . .	advanced to . . .
was given a raise . .	earned a raise . . .
my task was monthly reconciliation of . . .	reconciled monthly . . .

Note how strong verbs often eliminate the need for connectives. Watch connectives because they entangle. Avoid particularly triple-headed prepositions like *with regard to, in regard to, in connection with,* and *by means of.* Instead of "answered letters in connection with (with regard to, in regard to) complaints by means of (through the medium of) adjustment letters," say "prepared adjustment letters to answer complaints." You could also simplify the triple-headed connectives and write "answered complaint letters with adjustment letters."

TIP
Avoid abbreviations.

Some resume writers try to conserve space through abbreviations. Never cram your resume with abbreviations, whether the abbreviations are standard or invented by you. It is better to write *Street* than *St.* and *June 1, 1971 to January 8, 1972* than 6/1/71 to 1/8/72. Do not add *-th* or *-rd* to number streets and dates. Always precede names with a title of courtesy—Mr., Ms., Miss, Mrs., Dr., or Professor.

Avoid especially invented abbreviations. Never write "Bal'd bks EOM, rep'd var'n'c's to Off. Mgr." for "Balanced books at end of month and reported variances to Office Manager."

TIP
Keep similar coordinate elements parallel.

Parallelism is placing similar, coordinate elements in the same grammatical package. Avoid the faulty parallelism exhibited in the column to the left below:

Faulty Parallelism	Improved Parallelism
Studied elementary and advanced physics	Studied elementary and advanced physics
High score on mechanical dexterity	Scored high in mechanical dexterity
Excellent in all demonstrations as rating achievement	Achieved excellent rating in all demonstrations.

The first entry in the faulty column is a verb phrase; the second a noun phrase; and the third an adjective phrase. All entries in the improved column are verb phrases. The strongest entry you can make in presenting your educational and experience qualifications is the verb phrase. A verb phrase is dynamic and shows you in action. Avoid adjective and adverb phrases; they detract from objectivity and credibility of the resume.

Do not mix noun phrases and verb phrases in the same series.

Noun Phrases and Verb Phrases Mixed	Noun Phrases
1970-1978. Worked as Chief Clerk	1970-1978. Chief Clerk
1969-1970. Processing Clerk	1969-1970. Processing Clerk
1968-1969. Performed duties as Clerk-Typist	1968-1969. Clerk-Typist

SECTION 4

THE COVERING LETTER

WHAT IS A COVERING LETTER?

Most resumes are mailed to the prospective employer under the cover of a letter. This *covering letter* applies for a specific job, arouses interest and desire by referring to the enclosed resume, and requests an interview. Since it applies for work, the covering letter is also called an *application letter*.

The covering letter is actually a *sales letter*. It sells you to the prospect, calling his or her attention to the qualifications summarized in the resume and thus motivating him or her toward sales action. As a sales letter, the covering letter is best built upon the sales cycle of *attention, desire, conviction,* and *action*.

Sales Cycle	Covering Letter
ATTENTION	Dear Dr. Smith:
The letter is addressed to an individual. It avoids the stereotype "This is in reply to your advertisement in ..." It offers the writer's main qualifications as an answer to reader's problems.	Two features of the technologist's position you advertised in today's *Atlanta Journal* suggest that I may be the assistant you are seeking: • eight years of general medical technology experience; and • interest in radioisotope specialization. As you can see in the resume I enclose, I meet both of these qualifications.
DESIRE	Registered with the American Society of Clinical Pathologists since 1970, I now have charge of all technology at a 125-bed hospital. I direct the work of two medical technicians and report directly to the clinical pathologist.
The interest aroused in the opening is converted into desire by stressing resume items that relate to specifications in help wanted advertisement. The power of the resume is advanced to support letter.	
CONVICTION	My interest in radioisotopes, which I mention in my resume objective, started in 1973 when I was a technologist with the Richmond Hospital of Physicians and Surgeons. I have continued my study of radioisotopes since that time. My present post is
Continuing to describe and to introduce resume items, the writer introduces conviction material. The reader is assured that the interest in radioisotopes is a deep one. The reason for wanting to change jobs is tied into the	

167

interest in radioisotopes. The promise of high recommendations convinces reader that all writer states is true.

highly satisfactory, but offers no opportunity for work with radio-isotopes. Dr. Carlsen, my superior, promises the highest recommendations.

ACTION.......................May I call upon you sometime soon

The action requested should always be an interview. You must have an interview anyway. A prospective employer is much more likely to respond favorably to an interview request. Make it difficult for the prospect to turn you down. Avoid vague endings like "If interested, please let me know."

and show you as well as tell you why I would like to work with you at Brand Memorial Hospital. Wednesday is my free day, but I could arrange to see you any day you find convenient. You can write to me or telephone me directly at the hospital (123) 654 0987, if you choose.

Tips for Composing the Covering Letter

Research makes possible a number of tips for composing the covering letter. Let us add these tips to those we have listed for the resume itself.

> **TIP**
>
> Never mail a resume without a covering letter.

You may hand a resume to a prospective employer at the beginning of an interview. You may send a resume to a prospective employer through some third party—say, a friend or a placement director. But when you mail a resume, always accompany it with a covering letter.

> **TIP**
>
> Address by name the individual with power to interview and hire you.

A covering letter is always prepared for some individual. Never run off a set of form letters to accompany your resumes. Find out who is responsible for hiring in the firm you address, if you don't already know. Prepare a special covering letter adapted to him and to the occasion. Write his name, title, and address at the head of the letter and include his name in the salutation—*Dear Mr. Jones.*

If you are answering a blind advertisement (one that gives a post office box number, but no names of individuals or company), you cannot address an individual. But you can adapt the letter to the specifications of the want ad.

If you know the name of the company, however, you can generally find the name of the person hiring. Call the firm and ask the operator for the name you want; be sure to get the spelling and title right. Or consult one of the directories listed in the Appendix of this book.

> **TIP**
>
> Plan your letter before you write it.

You will write better covering letters faster if you begin with a plan. Take a piece of scratch paper and make a few notes that help you see the job opportunity clearly. Strike a balance sheet like the one discussed on page 000, matching your qualifications with job requirements. Jot down other conditions you must consider when you write your letter. Use a scratch outline to plot the paragraphs of your letter. Incorporate into this plan some of the tactics covered by the other tips in this chapter. Write a note or two to cover first-paragraph attention. Write a note or two covering the development of a strongest selling point, if that seems best for a second paragraph. Plan your third paragraph. And your fourth and fifth, if you have them. Plan a last paragraph requesting an interview.

A letter plan can be very simple, but it will make a vast difference in the effectiveness of the covering letter. Here is a letter plan for the medical technologist's letter, exhibited earlier in this chapter.

Paragraph 1. Two features—want ad—
  • 8 yrs gen hosp exp.
  • interest isotope
Paragraph 2. Registered ASCP, now full charge
  125-bed hosp.
Paragraph 3. Interest began 1973 at Richmond, continued, present job highly sat.
  Dr. C will recommend.
Paragraph 4. Request interview, can call day off, anytime. Call at hospital.

TIP
Adapt the letter carefully to conditions of job opportunity.

You are hired for a job because you meet certain conditions better than anyone else applying. An employer has a problem to be solved and he needs a certain kind of employee to solve it. To find that employee, he establishes conditions which must be met by the applicant he chooses. Some of these conditions are fairly obvious; he wants an employee with a certain background, certain training, and certain experience. Some of these conditions are very special — say, patience with youngsters or knowledge of Spanish.

When you write a covering letter, you must always show how your qualifications meet the conditions of the job opportunity. Your resume summarizes many of your qualifications in terms of your job objective. Your covering letter must show specifically how items of your background match both the obvious and special conditions of that job. Stress in that letter main items of education and experience— say, a degree in statistics and experience in research—and also special qualifications for the job advertised—say, fluency in conversational Spanish.

Invited Letters. When an application letter is *invited,* conditions are usually stated in the want ad or the instructions given to an employment agency. An *invited letter* is one like the medical technologist's letter; it responds to a request for applications issued by an employer.

Knowing the conditions of job opportunity from the want ad and from her knowledge of clinical pathology, the medical technologist matched details from her

169

resume to job requirements. She adapted her letter carefully to show that she was the applicant the pathologist had in mind when he advertised for an assistant. Reread this letter and note how carefully it is adapted to job opportunity.

Uninvited Letters. When an application letter is *uninvited,* adaptation is more difficult. An *uninvited (prospecting)* letter is written when an applicant feels that a certain firm may need his services. Say, the applicant is a research analyst. He knows what kinds of firms employ research analysts. Naturally, he responds to want ads, if he can find them. But he also sends out his resume under the cover of uninvited letters to firms that do not advertise. A dedicated job campaigner explores all avenues to employment.

The uninvited letter must be adapted to a reader who does not expect a covering letter and resume. It must catch his attention without referring to conditions listed in a want ad or other invitation. It must direct his attention to the possibility of a vacancy and establish some of the conditions to be met by the ideal applicant. Finally, it must show how the writer has qualifications that make him the ideal applicant.

Consider, for example, a training supervisor who feels that a certain bank may need his services. After a little research in the bank's annual report and the *American Banker,* he wrote the following letter:

> Letter addressed to officer in charge of hiring, name learned through telephone call. Reader is given title of courtesy—*Mr.* Position of reader indicated—Vice-President.

Mr. Arthur C. Del Soto
Vice President
Metropolitan National Bank
709 Central Avenue
New York, New York 10090

Dear Mr. Del Soto:

> The reader does not expect this letter. The writer must arouse his interest without the advantage of a prepared reader's mind. The quotation appeals because it is lively and because it focuses a real problem in the reader's life.

"Today's bank training supervisor is one-half professional teacher, one-half professional banker, and one-half creative genius. It may not be good arithmetic but it's the truth. Where do we find this anomaly?"

When Mr. Terrence Fitzpatrick, Vice President in charge of Personnel, First National Bank of Hampton, uttered these words at the ABA Convention last month, his audience laughed, applauded, but shook their heads. The question was an apt one: where does one find this anomaly?

> Writer adapts further by quoting an individual the reader probably knows, an individual in a position very similar to that of the reader. In citing a statement at a banking convention, the writer demonstrates his own high interest in banking.

> This letter must be written in full detail because the reader must be sold on (a) his need for a training supervisor and (b) his need for this particular applicant.

170

> Writer moves from a problem seen as reader sees it to himself as a solution to that problem.

> Writer introduces resume, citing material that should interest reader.

Although I do not consider myself a genius—creative or otherwise—my experience and training make me that anomalous figure—today's bank training supervisor. As you can see in the resume I enclose, I have had seven years of solid experience as a bank training coordinator, designing courses, supervising teachers, buying materials, and writing manuals. Not the least of my challenges has been one of personnel development, both standard and opportunity.

> Not knowing specific interests of his particular reader, writer ranges items of background that may hit reader at his core of needs.

Nor is it a happenstance that I applied my training as a professional teacher to business or that I became interested in employee development. As you will note in my resume, I am a trained teacher of business subjects with a master's degree in psychology.

> Writer enters conviction stage, showing that employee development is a career interest. He cites specifics of education.

> Writer calls for action. Since he places himself on a professional plane, he does not high-pressure this call to action.

Perhaps I am that educator-bank training supervisor that you need in your bank. I would be very happy to call upon you at your convenience and discuss the possibility of putting my education and experience to work in your bank. Please let me know when it is convenient and I will make it my business to be there.

Whether the letter you write is invited or uninvited, interpret your qualifications into terms that solve his problems.

TIP
Open with an idea that captures attention and leads to your strongest selling point.

The opening and closing paragraphs are the key points of the covering letter. The opening must convince the prospective employer that the whole letter and the resume enclosed are worth reading. The closing must motivate the prospective employer to interview action.

A good opening captures attention in a way that focuses your strongest selling point. The idea and phrasing of the opening must be arresting. Your reader may be screening hundreds of letters or he may be preoccupied with many other duties. Only the letters that capture his attention will be read. But this opening must transform attention into interest and desire by flashing as early as possible the great benefit you offer the reader.

Avoid the Stereotype Opening. You will increase by ninety percent the chances of being read if you avoid trite openings like the following:

- This is in answer to your advertisement for an assistant bookkeeper in today's *Star Dispatch*.
- Your advertisement for an assistant bookkeeper caught my eye as I read today's *Star Dispatch*.
- Do you need an assistant bookkeeper who is experienced, hard-working and honest? I happened to notice your ad for one in today's *Star Dispatch*.
- Thinking that you may need a bookkeeper, I am writing this letter to you.

Make the First Five Words Strong. The opening phrase can make or break your covering letter. Never begin with a dull idea or cliché phrasing. When you answer a newspaper advertisement, you invariably refer to the want ad, but you must never open with that want ad reference. Note in the first example below how reference to the want ad appears at the end of the sentence.

Generally, one of the three openings which follow places an interesting idea in the first phrase of a covering letter.

1. The Strongest Selling Point (Big Benefit) Opening

Sometimes your strongest selling point provides the best possible opening. Ask yourself, "Why should Mr. Jones hire me?" The answer is your strongest selling point, "Because I'm experienced in marketing research, trained in statistics, and fluent in Spanish." Open your covering letter with this selling point, if you can.

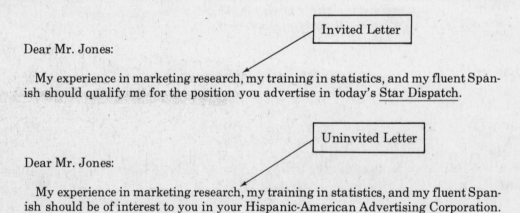

Dear Mr. Jones:

> My experience in marketing research, my training in statistics, and my fluent Spanish should qualify me for the position you advertise in today's <u>Star Dispatch</u>.

Dear Mr. Jones:

> My experience in marketing research, my training in statistics, and my fluent Spanish should be of interest to you in your Hispanic-American Advertising Corporation.

2. The Arresting-Idea Opening

Sometimes you must open with an idea that is primarily an attention getter. Your strongest selling point may not fit the opening paragraph or it may not have enough attention-getting appeal for your reader. Once you capture attention you can bridge into your strongest selling point. The training supervisor's letter on page 170 used an

172

arresting-idea opening; this interesting quotation bridged easily into the applicant's strongest selling point.

The secret of the arresting-idea opening is choosing an idea that relates to your strongest selling point. Consider the credit manager who applied for a position with a cosmetics manufacturer. In his research he found that the president of the company had been a psychology major in college and often attributed his success to the application of psychology to business. Capitalizing on this knowledge, the credit manager opened his letter with an attention-getting idea:

Dear Mr. Smith:

"Character counts more than capital or capacity!"
These famous words of a great American financier are truer today than they were when first uttered forty years ago. As a credit manager I have built my success on character analysis. I am concerned with capital and with capacity, but my first concern is always character. I look first at the man and ask, "What's he like? How does he think? How does he act?"

3. The Name Opening

Sometimes the name of an influential person, known to both you and your reader, provides the best possible opening you can use.

Dear Mr. Brown:

Mr. Francis X. Anderton, President of Teton Industries, suggested I write to you about an opening you have for a systems designer. As a management intern with Roger, Pellett, and Rogers, systems consultants, I helped design and install the system now used at Teton. Mr. Anderton was most complimentary about my work.

> **TIP**
>
> Tap the power of your resume.

When you develop your strongest selling point and your various supporting points, draw attention to your resume. Note how the medical technologist's letter exhibited at the beginning of this chapter referred easily and logically to her resume twice. In the second paragraph, she said, "As you can see in the resume I enclose." In the third paragraph, she said "which I mention in my resume objective." References to resume bring the full power of that resume into play.

You do not have to comment on more than one or two resume items to tap the full power of your resume. But make those references specific. Never refer vaguely to the resume.

Vague, Hence Faulty	Specific Reference
Note in my resume how I qualify for a supervisor's post in electronics.	Note in my resume how I rotated yearly to a different technical department at Margrave, always serving as a unit supervisor and trouble-shooter.

The mission of the covering letter and resume is to gain an interview. Ask for an interview. Make it as easy as possible for the reader to grant the interview. Name times that are convenient. Make it difficult for the reader to refuse the interview. Never leave the matter vague. Note how the medical technologist's letter and the training supervisor's letter both pressed hard for an interview in the last paragraph.

If you are writing to a firm in some other part of the country, the problem of a interview may be awkward. But you must still request an interview. Perhaps you can call at a regional office. Perhaps the personnel person will visit a city near you. Perhaps you plan to visit the reader's city. If the reader encourages you to visit him, he is highly interested in you. Often he will finance the trip.

Phrase your covering letter in the simple, direct language of everyday speech. Avoid the "as per" and "pursuant to" expressions that some writers use to sound official. Avoid the triteness that makes many application letters dull. There are certain expressions you should avoid in your resumes and covering letters:

DON'T USE . . .

Awaiting the pleasure of a favorable response.
Full opportunity to display my performance capacity.
Attached herewith is my resume.
Please find enclosed my resume.
In this endeavor I was eminently successful.
Trusting you will give this application due and favorable attention.
Along the lines of.
And oblige the undersigned.
If you have any questions, please do not hesitate to ask.

Assume the reader's viewpoint. Imagine that you are the prospective employer reading that letter and resume. Would that letter sell you? Why? Why not?

Check the total impact of the letter and resume. Does the letter state or imply that you are looking for a specific job? Does the letter catch the reader at a point of interest, develop some strong selling points, offer proof, and call for an interview?

Check the tone of your letter. Is the tone confident and firm, without touches of conceit, selfishness, or brashness? Is the tone modest, without faintheartedness?

Check the mechanics, typing, and grammar. If you find typographical errors, correct them. Rewrite the letter if necessary. Verify the spelling of questionable words. Remember, most readers use spelling as an index to intelligence. Consider the punctuation. Have you used a comma where a period or semicolon is needed? Read the letter aloud. Does it sound grammatical? Ask a relative or friend to check the letter for you.

The covering letters on the pages that follow provide models to guide you in composing your letter. Apply the tests, outlined above, to these letters. Note how these letters carry out the tactics summarized in this chapter. Feel the spirit of these letters and transfer that spirit to your own.

65 Ocean Avenue
Brooklyn, New York 65432
March 23, 1980

Mr. Thomas Gallagher
President
Gallagher Products Company
1234 Poseidon Boulevard
Brooklyn, New York 65433

Dear Mr. Gallagher:

Perhaps I am the "one gal to the rescue" you seek in your "One Guy or One Gal to the Rescue" advertisement in today's Brooklyn Examiner. I'm a one-gal office force, ready to pitch in as early as next week if necessary. I have the solid experience you specify and I know my "way around the bases" of the one-gal office.

As you will note in the resume I enclose, my present employer is moving to South Jersey. Mr. Cunningham, the proprietor of the Manhattan Beach Metal Company, asked me to continue with the firm, but I do not want to leave Brooklyn. The details of your advertisement suggest to me that office conditions at Gallagher Products Company are very similar to those at Manhattan Beach Metal.

In addition to the planning, administering, payroll, bookkeeping, and all-points office duties I outline in my resume, please note that I have the "some college" you mention as probably helpful. My forty-five credits at Brooklyn College include psychology and economics as well as business skills.

Knowing how busy you are without your gal friday, I will call you in a few days. Or if you agree, upon reading my letter and resume, that I am the gal you need, call me at the home number listed in the resume or at Manhattan Beach Metal (456 0987). Please let me know when it would be convenient to see you. I'll be there.

Sincerely yours,

Writer adapts to the tone of want ad. She is brisk and lively and quotes from ad.

Writer develops as strongest selling point the fact that she now performs the required duties in an organization very similar to that of the prospective employer.

THIS LETTER ACCOMPANIES
RESUME ON PAGE 73

176

356 Arlington Street
Arlington, Virginia 09876
August 28, 1978

Mr. Arthur MacMahon
Personnel Director
Falmouth Stores, Inc.
Triton, Virginia 09877

Writer opens with strongest selling point.

Dear Mr. MacMahon:

My twenty-one years as a detective (sergeant) with the New York City Police Department and my ten years experience as an Assistant Director of Security with Patoma Warehouse Corporation should qualify me for the position of Security Director you advertise in today's Washington Ledger.

The resume I enclose for your convenience outlines all of the details of my experience and education. My investigations for the New York City Police Department, you will note, earned me five citations. My leadership and administrative ability can be judged from my present duties of assigning and rotating security personnel and the fact that I served as a sergeant in both the U.S. Army Military Police and the New York City Police Department.

Although I am very happy in my present job and Patoma is fully satisfied with my work, I feel that I am ready to assume full responsibility as a Security Director.

May I discuss my qualifications more fully with you at some time you find convenient? My home is just fifteen minutes from your office. I can see you any time during your regular office hours, since I work evenings with Patoma.

Please let me know when it is convenient and I will be there.

Sincerely yours,

Writer emphasizes two items of resume stressed as important in want ad—investigative and administrative experience.

THIS LETTER ACCOMPANIES RESUME ON PAGE 97

20 Wilbur Way
Parsons, Vermont 09876
September 21, 1978

Mr. Patrick C. Parkinhurst
Parkinhurst & Crandall, Architects
580 Broad Street
Columbus, Ohio 67890

This uninvited letter catches attention at a point of reader interest.

Dear Mr. Parkinhurst:

The beautiful First Federal Savings building you designed for Hampton Hills, Vermont, impressed me for one reason—it dovetails perfectly with the ethos of Hampton Hills. I am writing to you because my main objective as an architect is to associate with a firm that gives ethos of community such high priority when it designs a building.

At present, as you will note in the resume I enclose, I am associated with Green Lakes Corporation as a Supervising Architect. This position affords me very heavy experience with multi-story office buildings in all fifty states and in Puerto Rico. I confer with planning boards, prepare designs, perform general architectural duties, and oversee construction through a staff of five assistant architects.

Green Lakes is highly satisfied with my services, but I feel that I would be much happier working for an architectural firm rather than as an architect with a building company. My work with Green Lakes and the Travers Construction Company has grounded me thoroughly in the practical problems of building. As you will note in my resume, the Army trained me thoroughly in structural engineering. Carefully tailored design, like that of First Federal of Hampton Hills, is my great professional interest.

May I meet with you sometime soon and discuss more fully my desire to become associated with Parkinhurst & Crandall? Next week I will be in Dayton and the week after in Marion. Perhaps it would be convenient for you if I visited you in Columbus during one of those visits. Please let me know. It would be most satisfying to work for the firm that designed First Federal of Hampton Hills.

Sincerely yours,

This letter from a professional applicant maintains a professional tone through longer sentences and fuller reasoning.

THIS LETTER ACCOMPANIES RESUME ON PAGE 16

APPENDIX

For your convenience and further guidance, the following material is presented in this appendix.

TWO SPECIMEN OCCUPATIONAL WORKSHEETS
A DECISION TREE COMPARING TWO CAREER COURSES
AN ANNOTATED BIBLIOGRAPHY OF JOB REFERENCE BOOKS

TWO SPECIMEN OCCUPATIONAL WORKSHEETS

An occupational worksheet, as explained in Section 2, is a private, fully detailed summary of *all* your work qualifications. An effective occupational worksheet is *never* shown to a prospective employer because it carries confidential data that a careerist gathers for his own guidance. All the data you need for building a resume, writing application letters, or conducting an interview is stored in your occupational worksheet.

OCCUPATIONAL WORKSHEET OF CHARLES R. STONE—MAY 31, 19——

49 Alvirtine Boulevard   (201) 338-5617
Elizabethtown, New Jersey
07008

Personal Details

Date and Place of Birth: May 15, 19——, Hoboken, New Jersey

Height and Weight: 5′ 9″; 154 pounds

Health: Excellent

> My excellent health makes it possible for me to work long hours indoors or outdoors. I am very seldom ill and I can work on six or seven hours sleep. My health and stamina would permit my working days and attending college evenings.

Family: I am single, but expect to become engaged within a year. I live with my father, mother, and three older brothers; our family is close-knit and very happy. My father is a plumber.

Concept of Self: I consider myself hardworking, serious, and above average in intelligence. I like hard work and know that I can be successful in any field touching on the mathematical and mechanical, working alone or with people. I was once very shy, but most people thought my shyness was modesty. I feel that this shyness has disappeared. I like people and like to work with them; they say I inspire confidence.

179

Background Summary

I was born in Hoboken, New Jersey, but my family moved to Elizabethtown when I was one year old. My father has worked for plumbing and building contractors for thirty years, installing the plumbing in many housing developments of North Jersey. My three brothers are also plumbers, but I do not want to work in a building trade. I worked part-time and summers as a builder's helper all through high school and showed aptitude in carpentry, masonry, painting, electric wiring, and plumbing, but I would rather work in banking or retailing.

In high school I earned exceptionally high grades in mathematics, science, manual training, mechanical drawing, and music. My part-time work kept me from engaging seriously in athletics, but I played varsity football and baseball in my junior year.

My engagement to Mary Van Sears will be announced in June and we will be married within the year. I have known Mary since I was a child. Mary's father is a building contractor and a director in a savings and loan association. He showed me the advantages of a banking career and has influenced my career decision. I know that I would be very happy in banking.

Career Objectives

First Career Objective: To become a bank executive in North Jersey or in New York City.

Immediate Job Goal: A clerical position with a bank large enough to provide the advancement I desire.

Second Career Objective: A trained position with a retail organization large enough to provide the advancement I desire.

Comment: Mary's father called a banking career to my attention, but I've always wanted to work for a bank because bank work is clean and respected and because I'm quick at figures. My experience in the building trades showed me that I do not want to work with my hands and that banking is very important in financing the growth and prosperity of the community. A bank would pay my tuition at the university. Alternatively, I could take a job in retailing because several jobs are available and I could advance happily in that field if I worked hard. Either career would permit my marrying within a year; Mary would work for a while in her position as a secretary with the Public Service Gas and Electric.

Banking is my first choice of career, by far.

Career Timetable

Target Dates	Positions	Preparation Needed
1979	Become Bank Clerk	High school completed
1980	First Clerk	Take basic AIB courses
1981	Section Head	AIB courses and company training courses
1982	Section Head	Matriculate at university for BS in banking and finance Transfer AIB credits
1983	Section Head	Continue evenings at university
1984	Platform Assistant	Continue university
1985	Platform Assistant	Continue university
1986	Platform Assistant	Continue university

1987	Assistant Manager	Complete university; take bank manager's course in company training program
1988	Assistant Manager	Take advanced banking courses; Study banking independently
1989	Assistant Secretary	Continue study

Limitations

Mary and I both have strong family ties in North Jersey, and I would like to stay in the Metropolitan Area if possible. Mary will work for a year or two as we get started, but we could manage if our family expands. Mary's father would keep us through emergencies.

I will need a college degree to attain my ultimate goal of bank executive, hence; I will have to work where college is available. Most of the banks in this area grant tuition remission to their employees.

It will be advantageous to get a job in North Jersey or New York City.

Education and Training

- Public School 5, Elizabethtown, New Jersey, September 19——-June 19——

- Elizabethtown High School, Elizabethtown, New Jersey, September 19——-June 19——.

    Academic Course: "A" in all mathematics, science and history subjects; "B" in all English courses and other language courses. Took typing and bookkeeping as electives, earning "A" in both courses. Received honors or high honors every term.

    Extracurricular Activities: Played varsity football (halfback) and varsity baseball (third base) in junior year. Class president in sophomore, junior, and senior years and vice-president of student council in senior year. Outside employment curtailed extracurricular activities.

    Personal relations with faculty and other students:
    Enjoyed excellent personal relations with faculty and students. Mr. Alvin Gorman, principal, said he would give very high commendation. Mr. Arthur Adler, chairman of the Mathematics Department, promised also to give me high endorsement.

- Building Trades Apprentice Program Academy, Newark, New Jersey. Summers 19—— and 19——.

    Apprentice Certificate. While working summers in home building, I attended Building Trades Apprentice Program Academy in Newark during July and August 19—— and 19——. I scored superior in all areas including Blueprint Reading; Fundamentals of Carpentry, Plumbing, and Electricity; and Elementary Surveying.

181

Work History

Part-time
May, June,
September, and
October 19——

Full-time
July-August
19——

Bolivar Construction Company,Clifton, New Jersey.
Bolivar Construction Company was a $1,500,000 company. In 1976 it was absorbed by Mackingtosh Building and Supply, Inc., Barrington, New Jersey.

Position Held: General Helper

Worked as errand boy and handyman, but often permitted to help carpenters, bricklayers, plumbers, and electricians. I was considered a good worker by all. The job was valuable in showing me that I have high structural imagination, manual dexterity, and the ability to get along with supervisors and workers.

Mr. Thomas Spielmann, Manager of Bolivar Construction, is now employed by Kew Forest Construction, 140 Broadway, Yonkers, New York. My father still does occasional work for Mr. Spielmann. Mr. Spielmann promised to give me a good reference and arrange some interviews with some bank executives he knows.

Part-time
May, June,
September, and
October 19——
19——, and 19——

Full-time
July-August,
19——, 19——,
19——

Mackingtosh Building and Supply, Inc., Barrington, New Jersey. Mackingtosh Building and Supply is one of the largest construction companies in New Jersey. It is capitalized at $5,000,000. This company contracts to build both industrial and residential buildings, but also operates a large building supply wholesale outlet in Barrington. It has branches in Camden, Newark, and Hackensack.

Position Held: General Helper; Supply Clerk; Carpenter's Apprentice.

Started as a General Helper in 19——, but assigned to lumber section in September of that year. Mackingtosh, which absorbed Bolivar, had a large lumberyard in Barrington. I piled and checked lumber, loaded trucks, and kept records. My knowledge of lumber grew rapidly and I joined the carpenter's union as an apprentice. This work showed me that I could be very successful in the building trades. Work in the lumberyard brought me into proximity with a large shopping center and gave me high interest in retailing.

Mr. Lou Evans, Foreman, Mackingtosh Building and Supply, promised to give me a good reference, attesting particularly to my clerical aptitude.

Part-time
after school
and Saturdays,
November-
December, March-
April, 19—— and
19——

Colfax Hardware Concession, Highway 46, Shopping Center,
East Paterson, New Jersey

Position Held: Sales and Stock Clerk

Helped Mr. Anthony Colfax during his two peak seasons.
Stacked shelves, checked and waited on customers.

This position showed me that I liked working with people better
than working with my hands and did gain their confidence very
easily. I enjoyed the surroundings of retailing and was offered
several jobs as manager trainee by Highway 46 Mart (an outlet
of Murphy Stores, Inc.) management.

Achievements

My main achievement to date has been my working constantly, accumulating two
thousand dollars in savings, earning high grades in school, and earning two varsity
athletic awards in high school.

Special Talents and Skills

My mechanical aptitude and careful observation provide me with carpentry skill
equivalent to that of a union journeyman. I am also highly skilled in electrical wiring,
plumbing, and masonry. Unfortunately, these skills do not contribute directly to my
banking career, but the knowledge of these trades would be useful in those areas of
banking that deal with construction loans.

Friends and Relatives Who Can Help

Most of my friends and relatives have influence in the building trades. However, Mary's
father, some of my former supervisors, and two of my schoolteachers could give me
valuable advice, provide contacts, and serve as references if I enter banking.

Mr. John Van Sears, Proprietor, Sabbatini Construction Company,
   45 Carteret Drive, Elizabethtown, New Jersey 07008
Mr. Thomas Spielmann, General Manager, Kew Forest Construction
   Company, 140 Broadway, Yonkers, New York 13456
Mr. Lou Evans, Foreman, Mackingtosh Building and Supply,
   45 Liberty Street, Barrington, New Jersey 07009
Mr. Anthony Colfax, Proprietor, Colfax Hardware Concession, Highway 46
   Shopping Center, East Paterson, New Jersey 07986
Mr. Alvin Gorman, Principal, Elizabethtown High School,
   56 Hauxhurst Avenue, Elizabethtown, New Jersey 07008
Mr. Arthur Adler, Chairman, Mathematics Department, Elizabethtown High School,
   46 Hauxhurst Avenue, Elizabethtown, New Jersey 07008
Mr. Arthur Adler, Chairman, Mathematics Department, Elizabethtown High School, 6
   Hauxhurst Avenue, Elizabethtown, New Jersey 07008

346 Red Cedar Terrace   339-6717
Columbus, Ohio 03456

Personal Details

Date and Place of Birth: December 26, 1922; Carmel, California

Height and Weight: 5'6"; 126 pounds

Health: Excellent

My friends say that I exhibit vitality and look ten years younger than I am. I feel young.

Family: I live alone in my own five-room house; my only relative is my sister Winifred who lives with her family at 57 Main Street, Carmel, California.

Concept of Self: I am a self-reliant, hardworking career woman, looking forward to retirement in ten years. I can manage important departments employing hundreds of persons. Employees consider me charismatic, but firm. I know how to manage both men and women. I can take wide, unemotional views of problems, but I am considered warm and generous. Sometimes younger employees think I am old-fashioned and a stickler for details, but the details are important in the departments I manage. Frankly, I was happier as an assistant manager to another executive; but I value the higher earnings I have made as a manager. Money is important to me. I have the security of my savings. I have traveled widely. When I retire in ten years, I want to live abroad for a few years. P.S. I would not be heartbroken to get a job as an assistant manager, rather than that of manager, even though it would be a step-down in prestige and self-esteem. I see myself also as a dedicated participant in Columbus civic life.

Background Summary

I was born and raised in Carmel, California, where my parents owned and operated a very successful retail shop. We were very comfortable and very happy, living in one of the best parts of town. My parents are both deceased, but my sister's husband still operates the shop. I own one quarter of the business.

During high school, I was active in all extracurricular affairs and graduated magna cum laude. I won a national shorthand contest in my senior year (along with state prizes in shorthand, typing, and bookkeeping) and the publicity of these awards gained me my first job as secretary to the Executive Vice President of the Caspian Corporation, an airplane manufacturer, Mr. Thomas Sanuk. The headquarters office of Caspian was located in San Jaime, California. While working for Mr. Sanuk I atttended San Jaime College, Evening Extension Division, earning a Proficiency Certificate in Accounting Management. Mr. Sanuk traveled extensively and relied heavily upon me as his home office contact. I won two major awards for suggestions.

When Mr. Sanuk retired, I was made a supervisor in the Machine Records Section of the Controller's Office. I advanced quickly and was appointed Internal Auditor when this section was expanded into Operational Auditing Services.

I accepted the attractive offer from Griffield Chemical to become Assistant Manager of their Contracts Department. Here I quickly earned a reputation for my ability to master and remember details. In 1968 I was made Manager of the Records Division of Griffield in Columbus. Something about Columbus, Ohio, inspired me and I became active in Columbus civic affairs. I attracted the attention of Mr. Gerald McCaffrey, the president of Apexal and he offered me the position of Marketing Director, which I accepted. I soon reorganized and expanded the Marketing Division of Apexal. Unfortunately, Apexal was absorbed by the Luminale Corporation. Rather than go to Chicago, I remained in Columbus where I established my own consulting company. My main client was the Griffield Company, for whom I worked for many years. I could build up my consulting company, but I would rather be part of a large organization, particularly one with a pension plan.

Career Objectives

First Career Objective: To get a high-paying managerial job with full pension rights with a central Ohio corporation, to work for ten years and then retire.

Immediate Job: Position of manager or assistant manager in a department that requires creativity, precision, detailed analysis, and problems involving people, accounting records, and statistics.

Comment: I would be very happy to go back to Griffield, but would do so only if Griffield held out the offer. I could continue as a consultant, but the Griffield account might end at a minute's notice. I could join a consulting firm bringing in my present accounts, but I don't really like consulting. The big target in my career now is comfortable retirement abroad.

Career Timetable

I want to retire with a comfortable pension in 19——.

Limitations

I am 55 years old. I could pass for 45, but I would not deceive anyone. Besides, the record that makes me desirable as a manager makes me 55 not 45.

I want to remain in the Columbus area for the next ten years. I am heavily committed to several civic enterprises.

Education and Training

Carmel High School, Carmel, California, graduated magna cum laude with diploma in commercial program, 19——. Won gold medal in national shorthand contest while student. Won both shorthand and typing state contests.

San Jaime College, Evening Extension Division, granted Certificate of Proficiency, with honors, in accounting and management, 19——. The following represent-ative courses were especially valuable:

Auditing Financial Statements

This course extended the insights I had gained in high school bookkeeping to the various accounting statements I was meeting on the job in the Caspian Corporation. It gave me a broad view of accounting processes as they culminated in financial statements. With this foundation, I studied accounting on my own and I learned all I could about accounting procedures in the Treasurer's Department and the Controller's Department of the Caspian Corporation.

Internal Auditing

This course provided the broad definition of internal auditing I needed to qualify as Internal Auditor in the Caspian Corporation. This course had a hinge to management, for the instructor constantly stressed the importance of control as a management function.

Work History

June, 19——
to
April, 19——

The Caspian Corporation, San Jaime, California

This large manufacturer of airplanes employed 17,000 at the time of my employment and was capitalized at $286,827,357.

Positions Held:

Secretary to Mr. Thomas Sanuk, Executive Vice President, June, 19——-January, 19——

Hired as stenographer but assumed all routines of Mr. Sanuk's office. Became home-base pivot point for Mr. Sanuk when Mr. Sanuk traveled. Held daily telephone conversations with him on major decisions, but made most routine decisions in his name. I studied both the treasurer's and controller's function firsthand in this office and combined these insights with my courses in San Jaime College, Evening Extension Division.

Supervisor, Machine Records Section, Controller's Department, January, 19——, January, 19——

Promoted from Secretary to Supervisor of Machine Records when Mr. Sanuk retired. I supervised eighty clerks through day and evening assistant supervisors. The design of this system grew from a suggestion I had made in the company suggestion system while I was secretary to Mr. Sanuk. My system was described in Business Methods Magazine, June 19——. This system saved the company $15,000 annually, according to Business Methods Magazine.

Internal Auditor, Controller's Department, January, 19——-April, 19—

Promoted from Supervisor of Machine Records to post of Internal Auditor when the Internal Auditing Section was expanded into Operational Auditing Service. The idea of an Operational Auditing Service came from another prize-winning suggestion I had made while still a secretary to Mr. Sanuk. My experience and my intensive study qualified me for the post of Internal Auditor. In this position, I also served as the first lieutenant to the Director of Operational Auditing Services and helped manage 300 employees.

April, 19——
to
April, 19——

The Griffield Chemical Company, San Jaime, California. This national processor and distributor of chemical and pharmaceutical products employed 31,000 persons and was capitalized at $936,622,000.

Positions Held:

Assistant Manager, Contracts Department, April, 19——-January, 19——

Invited by Mr. Ron Blankenship to join Griffield when Mr. Blankenship became Manager of Contracts Department at Griffield. Mr. Blankenship had been a member of the legal staff of the Caspian Corporation and had noted my ability to handle complex details at Caspian. Although Griffield management wanted an attorney for this position, Mr. Blankenship persuaded management that I would be preferable. I gained such mastery of contracting techniques and contract details that I conferred constantly with top-echelon Griffield management. Mr. Blankenship brought me to Washington whenever he testified before governmental agencies. I testified before government committees several times.

I was the administrator of this department. I designed all department procedures and supervised the work of 100 employees. Many of these were law school graduates.

Manager, Records Division, January, 19——-April, 19——

Appointed Manager of Griffield's Records Division when all corporate records were centralized at the Columbus, Ohio, plant. This post gave me direct command of 300 employees and direct supervision of the company's EDP data bank. I participated in the design of this company, working directly with the national management consulting firm of Rennes, Campbell, and Dundee. I implemented the design, recruited the operating cadre, and managed this operation, budgeted at one million dollars annually, for seven years.

April, 19—— to February, 19——	Apexal. This large Columbus, Ohio, paper products manufacturer employed 20,000 persons and was capitalized at $200,000,000. It was merged in 19—— with the Luminale Corporation and the functions of all Columbus offices were transferred to the Chicago headquarters of the company.
	Invited to join Apexal by Mr. Gerald McCaffrey, president of Apexal, I joined Apexal as Marketing Director. In this position I reported directly to Mr. McCaffrey and participated in second-echelon staff conferences. I directed the work of 200 persons; one third of these employees were professional specialists in research or advertising production. The work was challenging and creative. I earned the cooperation and respect of the staff, primarily from my ideas. When Apexal was absorbed by Luminale in 19——, I was offered a choice of two attractive positions at the Chicago head-quarters of Luminale—Manager of EDP Operations or Assistant Director of Marketing. I found life in Columbus so rewarding, however, that I elected to remain in central Ohio.
February, 19—— to Present	Marilyn P. Montgomery, Management Consultant, Columbus, Ohio. Opened my own consulting company with Griffield my main client. I could build up this practice and hire several retired executives as a staff. However, I would be much happier working for a large company as a manager or assistant manager in the central Ohio area.

Achievements, Honors, and Awards

My scrapbook of newspaper and magazine articles about my work as a manager and as a civic leader now occupies 35 pages. These articles go back to the time I won a national shorthand contest to the opening of my own consulting company. My scrapbook of letters of commendations from executives and public officials now consists of ninety pages.

Some representative achievements include:

June, 19——. Gold Medal (First Prize), National Shorthand Contest. (In that same month I also won the California shorthand and typing contest and placed second in the California bookkeeping contest).

October, 19——. $200 award for design of Machine Records System at Caspian Corporation. My system was adopted and I had the honor of implementing it and becoming the first supervisor, at the age of 21. I was praised by Business Methods Magazine in June 19——.

November, 19——. $500 award for suggesting an Operational Auditing Service. Later I became Internal Auditor and de facto assistant manager of the service I had suggested, at the age of 23.

March, 19——. Commendation from Anthony Griffield, Chairman of Board, Griffield Corporation for my assistance to Mr. Blankenship when he appeared before committees of the United States Senate.

August, 19——. Commendation from Mr. John Schreiber, Governor of Ohio, for my Chairmanship of the Scioto Valley Ecology Committee.

August, 19——. Elected Ohio Businesswoman of the Year.

August, 19——. Subject of laudatory article in Executive Woman—"In Ohio, She's Marilyn Our Marilyn."

Publications

"Development of Operational Auditing Services," Engineer Auditor, June 19——. Vol. II, #15.

"Centralizing International Records in a Single EDP Bank," Office Procedure Annual, January, 19——. Vol. IV, #20.

Travel

I have visited all parts of the United States on business or on vacation. I have visited Canada and Mexico many times. I have visited Europe five times. I like travel and plan to spend my post-retirement years in travel.

Professional Societies

> Executive Guild of America
> American Institute of Women Accountants
> Institute of Internal Auditors
> Society for the Advancement of Management
> Ohio Society for Industrial Executives

Friends and Relatives Who Can Help

(See list of 75 VIPs in VIP address book)

A DECISION TREE COMPARING TWO CAREER COURSES

A decision tree permits the spreading in space of alternative career courses. In Section 2, we discussed the building of a decision tree (page 123). We illustrated the discussion with the example of a young man who must decide between two job opportunities. Here in full is the decision tree as developed by that young man.

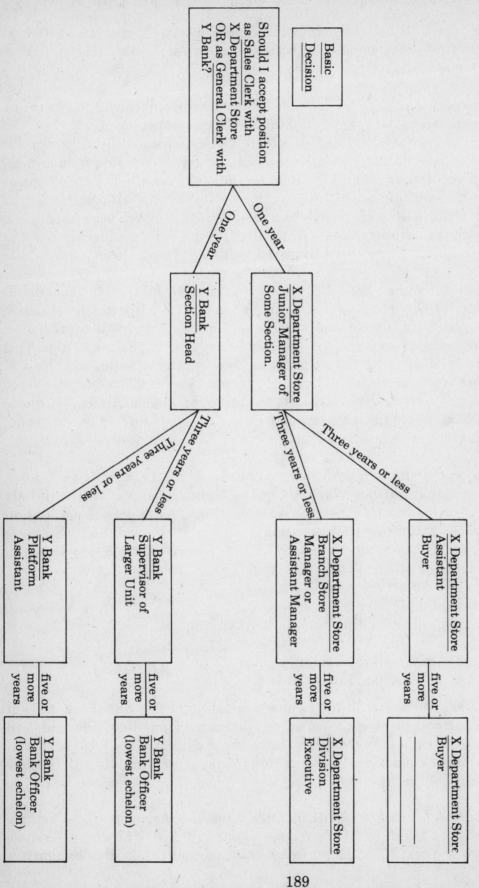

AN ANNOTATED BIBLIOGRAPHY OF JOB-REFERENCE BOOKS

The careerist works constantly with the following tool books and reference materials during job campaigns. You will find all these books in the reference sections of city public libraries.

- *Dictionary of Occupational Titles,* 2 volumes and supplement, published by U.S. Department of Labor, Washington, D.C. Acquaint yourself with this vast, definitive survey of jobs currently held in the United States. Leaf through the pages and note the many thousands of jobs described, ranging from *aircraft and engineer mechanic* to *zylor mounter* (an occupation in the optical goods industry). The exhaustive coverage of these volumes makes it possible for you to range the whole spectrum of jobs available and to match your talents and goals with the duties specified. Naturally, you cannot read the whole list of offerings, but browsing can prove most valuable.

- *Estimates of Worker Trait Requirements for 4000 Jobs as Defined in the Dictionary of Occupational Titles,* published by U.S. Department of Labor, Washington, D.C. Discover the specific information this guide furnishes on the more common jobs listed in the *Dictionary of Occupational Titles.* This book specifies training time, aptitudes, temperaments, interests, physical capacities, and working conditions. Under aptitudes it tells whether the job requires verbal, numerical, spatial, form perception, clerical perception, motor coordination, finger dexterity, manual dexterity, eye-hand-foot coordination, color discrimination, and intelligence.

- *Occupational Outlook Handbook,* published by U.S. Department of Labor, Bureau of Labor Statistics, Washington, D.C. Acquaint yourself with this fully definitive review of nearly two thousand job titles, ranging from *accountant* to *postal clerk.* Although not as exhaustive in job titles as the *Dictionary of Occupational Titles,* the *Occupational Outlook Handbook* provides full analysis of each job title listed, including:
  Nature of Work;
  Places of Employment;
  Training, Other Qualifications, and Advancement;
  Employment Outlook;
  Earnings and Working Conditions; and
  Sources of Additional Information.

The detailed guidance and the frequent updating of this handbook make it possible for you to range a selective spectrum of possible jobs and find answers to any questions you may have about each of these jobs. A special volume of the *Occupational Outlook Handbook* extracts and lists all the jobs that require college degrees.

- *Occupational Literature: An Annotated Bibliography,* edited by Gertrude Forrester, published by H.W. Wilson Company, 950 University Avenue, Bronx, New York, 10452. Now in its third edition (1971), this exhaustive bibliography identifies books, pamphlets, posters, leaflets, and other literature on job openings in a variety of fields. For example, it guides you to literature on such unusual jobs as *bee keeping* and *toe dancing* as well as to literature on more conventional jobs in business, industry, civil service, and the armed forces.

- *Thomas Register of American Manufacturers and Thomas Registry Catalogue,* published by Thomas Publishing Company, 461 Eighth Avenue, New York, New York, 10001. If you want to work for the manufacturer of some product—say, automobiles, baby food, cosmetics, or typewriters—consult this register. Each product and subproduct is listed and manufacturers are specified with names and addresses.

    Glancing through this volume, you may discover the kind of work you want to do in terms of a product. If you find an area of special interest, you can write to the manufacturers and request brochures on careers with that company. The brochures companies send are generally excellent, and often illustrated, describing jobs and duties performed in the companies, qualifications, chances for advancement and working conditions. Often these brochures give you insight to job titles you should know, like *cost accounting* and *systems analysis*. For example, the brochure of Standard Brands, Incorporated describes the position of *product manager,* a job that might be the kind of work you've always wanted.

- *Encyclopedia of Associations,* edited by Margaret Fisk, Gale Research Company, Book Tower, Detroit, Michigan, 48226. This guide gives you still another angle of approach to the job market, still another lead to helpful brochures. Glancing through Volume I of this guide, you review all the trade and professional associations that serve America. Each of these associations relates to an area of work. If any field—say, insurance actuarial work— appeals to you, write for literature to the associations serving that field. For example, the *Society of Actuaries* in Chicago or the *Casualty Actuarial Society* in New York will send you a sample actuarial examination. Here's a chance to see whether you have the mathematical skill needed to become an actuary.

- *College Placement Annual,* published annually by the College Placement Council, Incorporated, P.O. Box 2263, Bethlehem, Pennsylvania, 18001. Designed primarily for the new college graduate, this annual publication is a treasure trove of information for the young careerist. In addition to some helpful articles on job getting, it lists a large number of companies seeking young college graduates and describes jobs in these companies. It is well worth examining, whether you are a college graduate or not.

- *Moody's Industrial Manual,* published by Moody's Investment Service, 99 Church Street, New York, New York, 10007. This volume provides current information on American corporations, giving history, nature of business, property, expansion, and officers. It is valuable for surveying the job market by entries on specific corporations.

- *Poor's Register of Corporation Directors and Executives,* published by Standard and Poor's Corporation, 345 Hudson Street, New York, New York, 10014. Like Moody's, this volume permits an approach to the job market by specific corporations. It is invaluable as an up-to-date source on who manages each corporation, identifying by name board members and major executives.

Index

Doctor of Medicine (MD), 79
Doctor of Philosophy (Ph.D.), 42
Draftsman, 41
Dramatic coach, 88

Economic analyst, 18, 35, 42, 48
Economics major, 42, 45
Economist, 42
Editor, 29, 46, 81, 105
EDP specialist, (Electronic Data Processing), 30, 31, 38, 68, 69, 72, 109
Education entry on resume, 150, 154, 158-159
Education major, 100
Educator, 42, 88, 99, 107
Electrical engineer, 19, 29, 47, 102, 104, 105
Electrician, 60
Electronic Data Processing specialist (EDP), 30, 31, 38, 68, 69, 72, 109
Electronics industry experience, 11, 29, 30, 47, 85, 105
    See also Electronic Data Processing.
Employee training director, 67, 107
Employment counselor, 77
Encyclopedia of Associations, 191
Engineer, 19, 29, 47, 85, 102, 104, 105
Engineering designer, 41
English major, 59, 100
    See also Editor
Environmentalist, 16, 22, 39, 65, 178
Equal-opportunity specialist, 67, 99
Estimate of Worker Trait Requirements, 190
Estimator, 32
Executive secretary, 12, 96
Experience entry in resume, 150, 154-155, 158-159
Explore all avenues to job, 2-3, 170-171
Extracurricular activities, 151, 158
Eye movement in reading resume, 147

Factory foreman, 49, 51, 85
Family service counselor, 98
Figure clerk, 20, 26, 28, 76
File clerk, 26, 28
Finance major, 37, 48, 89
Financial analyst, 35, 48
Financial condition entry on resume, 42, 78, 160
Financial manager, 35
Finding name of person hiring, 168
Fine arts major, 17
Flow charting specialist, 30, 64, 69, 72, 102
Food-processing industry, 40, 49, 52, 58, 77, 90, 94, 101
Food-processing technician, 40, 58, 94
Foreman
    auto mechanic, 50
    construction, 32

factory, 49, 60
    mechanical, 50, 60, 106
Formats of resume, 150-156
Form letters of application
    avoid, 168
Foundation experience, 43
Foundation of resume, 129-162
Free-lance artist, 17
Full-charge bookkeeper, 11, 12, 23
Functional resume, 151, 155-156

Gal/guy Friday
    letter, 176
    resume, 12, 73
Gathering personal records, 111 ff.
General office worker, 15, 70
Goals
    immediate, 114 ff., 157, 180, 185
    long-range, 114 ff., 157, 180,. 185
Government experience, 40
Graphic-arts specialist, 17
Green card holder, (Permanent resident), 68
Group industrial leader, 51
Grouping resume data, 150-156
Guard and watchman, 56, 97
Guidance counselor, 67
    See also Counselor

Handicapped, teacher of, 122
Headings
    centered, 133-137
    cut-in, 36-38, 63-65, 134, 138-139
    side, 133-137
Headline in resume, 134, 147, 163-164
Health industry experience, 53, 66, 71, 79, 80, 88
Hobbies 151, 160
Home-economics, 52, 122
Honors and award entry on resume, 22, 53, 61, 62, 65, 72, 94, 160
Hospital administrator, 53
Hospital attendant, 40, 53, 66, 79
Hostess, 15
House organ editor, 29, 46, 105
Hung indention, 142, 145

Immediate job objective, 114 ff., 157, 180, 185
Indention
    hung, 142, 145
    paragraph, 142
Industrial designer, 41
Industrial foreman, 50, 51
Industrial group leader, 51
Industrial maintenance, 60
Industrial physician, 79
Industrial quality control, 85
Industrial relations manager, 77
Industrial salesman, 80
Information specialist, 46, 81
Information systems specialist, 30, 62, 102
Inside adjuster, 55
Insurance claims adjuster, 55

Insurance experience, 21, 46, 55, 72, 107, 108
Insurance specialist, 13, 48, 55, 108
Intern, 51, 59, 78
Internal auditor, 11, 19, 62
Interpreting
    experience, 112-114, 163, 181-182, 185, 187
    interpretative note in career analysis, 112-114
    military experience, 114
    on resume, 162-163
    personal record, 112-113, 163
    school and college courses, 112-113, 181
Interviewer, 18, 35, 67, 77, 98
Interviews
    application blanks and, 3
    out-of-town, 174
    request interview in covering letter, 168-169, 171, 174
    using resume in, 3
Inventory control manager, 12, 24
Inventorying self, 112-122
    See also Analysis
Investigator, 55, 56, 97
Investment analyst, 48
Invited applications, 2, 169-170, 176-177
Invited letter of application
    discussed, 169
    examples, 176, 177
    See also Covering letter

Jargon
    avoid, 163, 174
Job campaign, 2, 114, 124, 168-169
Job corps specialist, 67
Job goals
    immediate, 114 ff., 157, 180, 185
    long-range, 114 ff., 157, 180, 185
Job guidance counselor, 67
Job market, 2, 119 ff., 124
Job market analysis, 119 ff.
Job objective
    immediate, 114 ff., 157, 180, 185
    long-range, 114 ff., 157, 180, 185
Job satisfaction, 117-118
Journalism major, 29, 46, 105
Journalist, 29, 46, 81, 105
Journeyman, 33, 41, 50, 60, 106
Junior accountant, 11, 69

Keypunch operator, 30
Knowledgeability on job market, 119-120
Know thyself—Know thy work, 114-127
    See also Analyzing Self, 115 ff.

Labels
    data, 134, 139-140
Laboratory technician, 22, 58, 66
Labor relations manager, 49, 77

Ladies' shoe buyer, 24
Landscaper, 60
Law school graduate, 18, 68, 77
Lawyer, 18
Layout and visualization artist, 17
Layout person, 17, 33, 49, 106
Legal aide, 18
Letter of application
    as sales letter, 167–169
    composing, 168–169
    invited, 167–170, 176–177
    planning, 168–169
    uninvited (prospecting), 170–171, 178
Liberal arts major, 31, 45, 59, 79, 88, 95, 100
Librarian, 59
Library
    research for job and career, 120, 190-192
Licenses, professional, 78, 79, 86, 88
Line of data, 140–141
Lines used in resume, 12, 15, 16, 71, 146
List of occupations, 6–9
Loan administrator, 37
Lobbyist, 81
Locating name of person hiring, 168
Long-range career objectives, 114 ff., 157, 180, 185
Long-term job objective, 114 ff., 157, 180, 185

Machine assembler, 49
Machine repair person, 49, 50
Magazine editor, 29, 46, 105
Maintenance superintendent, 49, 50, 60
Management accountant, 19, 62
Management aide, 12, 61, 64, 72, 73, 96
Management consultant, 21, 31, 43, 63, 103
Management major, 51, 55
Management science specialist, 30, 62
Management trainee, 61, 89, 108
Manager
    Benefits and compensation, 21
    General, 62
    Office, 72
    Personnel, 77
    Records, 187
    Restaurant, 91
    Retail, 78
Manpower specialist, 67, 77
Manuals writer, 29, 65, 107
Manufacturer's representative, 94, 95
Margins of resume, 149
Market for jobs, 119–124
Market research manager, 24, 42
Marketing director, 13, 24, 63, 80
Marketing major, 13, 24, 83, 94
Marketing specialist, 13, 14, 24, 63, 80, 95
Mason, 60

Master of Arts (MA), 45, 67, 88, 100, 107
Master of Business Administration (MBA), 19, 35, 37, 48, 83, 85, 102, 104
Master of Hospital Administration (MHA), 54
Master of Library Science (MLS), 59
Master of Science (MS), 40
Matching qualifications to job demand, 120–122
Mathematician, 30
Mathematics major, 30, 45
MBA (Master of Business Administration), 19, 35, 37, 48, 83, 85, 102, 104
Mechanic, 50, 60
Mechanical engineer, 47, 85, 105
Media director, 13
Medical doctor, 79
Medical social worker, 98
Medical technologist
    letter, 167–168
    resume, 66
Merchandise manager, 24
Military service entry, 19, 34, 41, 45, 46, 49, 50, 54, 56, 77, 88, 92, 97, 100, 108, 160
Millwright, 49, 106
Minority manpower specialist, 67, 99
Model, 87
Mod-retail manager, 93
Moody's Industrial Manual, 191

Name of person hiring
    how to find, 168
Name-opening in covering letter, 173
New citizen or permanent resident, 68
Newspaper reporter, 29, 46, 81, 105
No-experience college graduate, 69
No-experience high school graduate, 70
Noncitizen or permanent resident, 68
Nurse, 71, 98

Objective, 114 ff., 157, 180, 185
Objectivity in resume, 162
Occult center, 148
Occupational Literature, 190–192
Occupational Outlook Handbook, 190
Occupational worksheet
    compared to resume, 130
    discussed, 2, 124–127
    example, 179–188
Office assistant, 15, 70
Office boy, 70
Office manager, 35, 62, 72
Office worker, 12, 15, 23, 28, 53, 61, 70, 72, 73, 87, 96, 101, 109
One-gal office, 12, 73
One-page resume, 131
Opening of covering letter, 167, 172–173

Operational auditor, 11, 19, 155, 162, 185 ff.
Operator
    business machines, 12, 26, 28, 57, 70, 73, 87, 109
    key punch, 30
    telephone (switchboard), 101
    word processor, 109
Optical center, 130, 147–148
Out-of-town interviews, 174
Overseas
    education, 68, 92,
    experience, 68, 72, 80, 83

Painter, 60
Paragraph data, 2
Paragraphs
    long data blocks, 142
Parallelism, 166
Paramedical aide, 53, 66, 98
Part-time work
    experience, 30, 55, 57, 59, 61, 73, 75, 87, 88, 108, 159
    how to show, 159
Payroll clerk, 76
Permanent resident (Green card), 68
Personal data entry, 143, 144, 157
Personal records, 111–113
Personal trust officer, 18, 48
Personnel manager, 67, 77
Pharmaceutical
    experience, 51, 78, 83, 95
    salesman, 95
Pharmacist, 78
Phi Beta Kappa, 22, 39
Photographs on resume, 134
Phrasing resume data, 162–166
Physical education teacher, 88
Physician, 79
Placement officer, 77
Planning
    covering letters, 168–169
    resumes, 132
Playground director, 88
Police officer, 56, 97
Poor's Register of Corporation Directors and Executives, 192
Portfolio analyst, 43, 89
Positive statements, 164–165
Post office box replies
    adapting letter to, 168
Press agent, 46, 81, 105
Principal, 99
Private accountant, 11, 35
Private duty nurse, 71
Private investigator, 56
Pro-and-con analyses, 121-122
Probing self, 112–113
Problem-solving approach, 169, 171
Procedures writer, 19, 29, 30, 31, 53, 65, 102 ff., 105
Product designer, 80
Product manager, 80
Production supervisor, 19, 47, 49, 51, 61, 62 ff., 80, 85